SUBSIDIARITY, LOCALISM, AND TRUE DEMOCRACY

SUBSIDIARITY, LOCALISM, AND TRUE DEMOCRACY

Paul Fairchild

SUBSIDIARITY,LOCALISM,ANDTRUEDEMOCRACY

iUniverse books may be ordered through booksellers or by contacting:

iUniverse
1663 Liberty Drive
Bloomington, IN 47403
www.iuniverse.com
844-349-9409

ISBN: 978-1-6632-4249-5 (sc)
ISBN: 978-1-6632-4248-8 (e)

Library of Congress Control Number: 2022918527

Print information available on the last page.

iUniverse rev. date: 10/04/2022

To Zelma Markwell, a wonderful teacher, guide, and inspiration.

CONTENTS

INTRODUCTION

This book explores the relationships between localism, subsidiarity, and true democracy and their contributions to peace. It draws on the history of the United States and the interpretation of that history including public information intended to influence its citizens to support policies and practices aimed not at the common good but at the good of the wealthy and powerful. Awareness of their activities and its consequences is becoming better known. This book aims to advance that awareness and enhance it with knowledge of its ethical dimension by bringing into the discussion a topic unknown to most Americans, that of subsidiarity. A moral principle, it requires that higher levels of power and authority refrain from establishing policy for their included lower levels unless the lower levels are unable to do so.

Given the current struggle between those who would increase democratic participation in the country and those who would reduce it to influence the outcome of voting in their favor, it is timely and needed to strengthen our understanding of how to make government serve the common good.

Introducing subsidiarity into the book's other topics will help readers balance the application of pragmatism and ethics in considering the subjects of the book, an ability we all need if we are to respect what the people of the US are capable of and desire in their social and political lives. Presenting it here and elsewhere will increase the number of people aware of it, concerned about its application, and working to make it a part of the future of democracy in the country.

I am motivated to apply my education in law and philosophy to be part of the movement underway to improve our and succeeding generations' lives. May the movement grow and continue to the point that it becomes an example taken up in other countries needing the same improvements as ours.

CHAPTER 1

The Myth of American Democracy

The history of the United States tells of an area of North America settled by European immigrants and their descendants, mainly from England, who created colonies operated primarily for the economic benefit of their country of origin.

As subjects of the British Empire and living in a locus of conflict, the colonists' growing desire for independence and self-government led to a revolution and the founding of a nation. This is the story we hear from childhood and throughout our lives about the origins of this country. The story stresses the part played by democracy in the thoughts of its founders and in the US Constitution they created.

The first three articles of that document confirm that truth. It describes a republic whose governing officials gained office by the vote of the people. They regularly faced competition with other candidates, elections being held every two years for members of the House of Representatives, every four years for a president and vice president, and every two years for a third of the members of the Senate, giving each a six-year term. That placed in the hands of citizens the power to determine who would lead and govern them from the national headquarters. As we are taught, it describes a democratic republic.

Yet there is a growing awareness that forces other than the will of the people play a more important role in determining our laws and policies. It is tempting to think we could simply identify the usurping forces and move the power from them back to the people, but that overlooks a more important problem we face. This book will show that the solution involves much more than a power shift and will require a major change in our understanding not only of the locus of political power in the country but also of flaws in its constitutional design.

We begin with correcting the story of America and the language used to tell that story. Political language hides the problem. Its use supports the assumption that the founders created a fully democratic state. As a result, the idea that America is such a democracy is almost universally accepted by its citizens. That acceptance needs to be challenged. I believe that Chalmers Johnson, the author of *Nemesis: The Last Days of the American Republic*[1] does challenge it and that there are other writers who do so but whose positions are overlooked.

The US is not a true democracy. How can we say that when we have elections regularly and a government whose leaders come from the elections? The move to elected leaders and away from monarchy occurred with the adoption of the Constitution. It set out the structure of a national government and its relation to the states. It provides rules for filling the offices of the presidency, the Senate, and the House of Representatives, and its amendments empower citizens to do so by voting. And yet those who claim that the word *democracy* fails to describe the US federal government have reason to do so.

---

[1] Johnson mentions many instances in the work of some presidents' lies to the American people and the secrecy of government that inhibit a major need for full democracy—an informed public.

As most American adults know, *democracy* comes from an ancient Greek word that describes the form of government of a city-state. It means rule by the people. It describes the form of government adopted in Athens, making the city-state an example to be followed just as its writings, arts, and architecture became models for other places and times. But a closer look at Athenian democracy merits attention if we are to understand why the application of the word there and in the United States has qualifications.

We should note that the Athenian form of democracy applied to a city-state. The American form of democracy applied from its beginning to the nation and covered the thirteen original states. Because of its smaller size, Athenians enjoyed direct democracy, the ability for each voter to have a voice and vote in political decision-making affecting them. The new US adopted a representative form of democracy, a form by which citizens elected others to represent them and who would, presumably, make decisions for them consistent with the good of the people and their wishes on particular political choices.

But not all citizens of Athens had political power. Only free males born there could vote. Women had no political power. Nor did slaves, who created much of the wealth the Athenians depended on. And even Aristotle, one of the most famous Greek philosophers, did not share political power in Athens despite his growing knowledge of politics since he had been born in Stagira in northern Greece. Even though he was Alexander the Great's teacher in Macedonia, that position did not lead to his being accepted as a voting citizen of Athens.

The historically first adopter of the idea of democracy did not create its full reality in what it established. Nor did it continue to rule without interruption by autocracy. We should recognize that so radical a change from earlier forms of government would take time, experience, and experimental changes to develop into a stable reality. And Athens's democracy was not stable. It ended with the Peloponnesian War, which left Athens crippled, and it did not rise elsewhere for a long time. Yet the idea and ideal of democracy lived on at least in the literature that survived the ages. And during the Enlightenment, it became a topic of further development. The authors who wrote about politics during that historically important period inspired others to take the form seriously and adopt it.

One of the most admired aspects of the American Revolution consists in its leaders taking the word of the Enlightenment writers and attempting to establish democracy as the form of government of the US. Having the example of ancient Greece and the desire to break away from England and its king, the founders of the new nation set out a plan with improvements over the previous attempt to create a stable form of government. And so far, the plan has worked. For over two hundred years, Americans have continued to elect their national, state, and local leadership with of course the exceptions of some appointive offices, the highest being the US Supreme Court. That it has continued for so long stands for many as proof of its merit.

Some other nations including those that chose a parliamentary form of democracy have done well. Theirs, like the Athenians' and ours, are experiments. We should not expect that something as complicated as a national government could be designed and formed to be perfect on the first try. It involves too many functions and purposes for that expectation to be realistic. That is not to say that we are unable to improve it. The goal of this book is to identify improvements that deal with the real problems of the current expression of democracy in America.

More Americans are learning that at its founding, the US shared some of the flaws of the Greek democracy. Political power in the new republic was not shared by all its adult residents. Native Americans, slaves, women, and some indentured servants were denied the right to vote.

Amendments to the Constitution corrected those flaws over time. The Thirteenth Amendment abolished slavery in 1865, and the Fifteenth Amendment in 1870 gave former slaves the right to vote while prohibiting its denial based on race or color. The Nineteenth Amendment in 1920 gave women the right to vote. Extending the right to vote to all adult citizens furthered the degree to which the US could properly be called a democracy. But the legal right to vote, unless practiced and allowed, must end up in its neglect and remain a major flaw of any democracy.

We have moved away from rule by the people to a degree, and in a way, that has harmed us and threatens the existence of the nation and to show that its stability, while long by some standards, has been lost. Think of what that would mean for other imperfect democracies.

In what way is democracy in America a myth? Unlike the ancient Greeks, women have the vote, there are no longer slaves kept from voting, and the foreign-born can become citizens with full voting rights. Yet we can truly say that the people do not rule the nation. We do not have a government of the people, by the people, and for the people. Political language in this country has many ways of disguising the true state of democracy and filling the dialogue with words we accept when their use hides the truth.

Take for example the word *patriotism*. It is often used to describe support for some political proposal or for service in the military, but its use overlooks the true meaning. Used correctly, patriotism refers to place, not to institutions. True patriotism means love of the place where one's ancestors lived, died, and are buried. That place cannot be as large as the globe or a giant territory as large as China, India, Russia, Europe, or the United States. The term originated in the Roman Empire but did not refer to love of the empire. It referred to the patria or fatherland, a local area where one had been born and desired to live out one's life because of what one's parents, grandparents, and other predecessors had done there and passed on. It was a shared virtue, a shared love of the land and its produce. Now, the term has been corrupted to refer to an institution, the national state. One indication of the imperfection of our use of the term appears when we refer to our military members as patriots but do not call the military members of nations we have fought patriots. We have lately come to refer to our military members as heroes as well and have even extended the use of that term to apply to anyone who wears a uniform, military or not. But those who wear uniforms in our enemy nations are not called heroes by us.

We also abuse the term *freedom*. Its true meaning is complex; it can refer to freedom to perform certain activities, freedom from certain controls or interferences, and freedom from harm. The value of political freedom has many facets, but freedom does not mean simply the right to do whatever one wants, a way the term is being used lately. Some use the term even when what one wants harms others. Freedom to act is and must be limited to behavior that does not harm others. Yet the term is being used to excuse not taking action to prevent the spread of COVID-19, as if the individual should be free to spread the deadly disease by refusing to be vaccinated and refusing to wear a mask around others. Such freedom benefits no one, not even those who claim to have it.

Even use of the term *democratic* has changed. A Democrat, a member of the Democratic Party, provides the noun to allow the brief reference to a person based on party loyalty. Now, we often hear opponents of the party, and particularly Republican leaders, using the term as if it has become an adjective. How often we hear such expressions as "the democrat bill," "the democrat craziness," or "a democrat plan." Because it refers to the Democratic Party, we should hear the word "Democratic" in the sentence. But apparently, its use that way is believed to suggest a fulfillment of democracy by the Democratic Party. And since the Republicans want to defend their interpretation of democracy and value the word, they replace its adjective with a noun. But there is no Democrat Party in the United States. It also shows that they either do not know or don't trust the public to know that when written, the word *democratic* refers to the form of government and *Democratic* refers to the political party.

Some others of our political terms suffer from lack of clarity. The American dream appears to apply to a state of mind of foreigners, would-be immigrants, to live a good life, easily found in the United States. But as many immigrants have discovered, the good life may not be achieved by crossing the border into the country. It seems to suggest great or at least adequate wealth and enjoyment of its benefits, something many in the US fail to experience. It supposedly derives from the freedom, democracy, and rights of individuals found in the US. Unless those ideals are true and manifest for all people, we must conclude that the dream is based on a wish, not on reality. Defining success as wealth promotes a competitive way of life that limits happiness for many people.

Another expression, America First, remains mysterious even after many years. I have never read or heard anything that answers the question "America, first what?" It apparently does not mean America first in time since its use seems to suggest some sort of ranking rather than its being the first nation-state. But its rankings in many desirable characteristics fall far below that of other developed nations. It was used by President Wilson to promote a foreign policy of nationalism and nonintervention in foreign states. It was used by the Ku Klux Klan to promote its racism. And Donald Trump used it to justify withdrawing from international treaties and organizations. Even if meant to suggest that America is the first among nations of the world in desirable characteristics, its use for that is wrong.

We should note first that the rankings of nations differ among those doing the rankings and the basis for comparison. The *US News and World Report* recently ranked Canada as the best country to live in and own a business. Because those doing the ranking use different standards and rely on different sources of fact and opinion for their conclusions, we might first decide on which one is most pertinent to this study before reporting its conclusions.

In a ranking of the quality of their governments as democracies, Denmark, Norway, Finland, and Sweden held the top four positions and were classified as working democracies while the US was ranked number 36 and was classified as a deficient democracy. The nations at the bottom of the list of 176 were classified as hard autocracies.[2] The UN ranks 189 of them on human development. It places Norway at the top and the United States in position 17.[3] It uses the HDI (Human Development Index). But that index, while based on lifespan and education level, also includes GNI (gross national income measured per capita). Such averaging hides high incidences of poverty when a few have extremely high incomes. This places the US and China in the top two positions.

The Heritage Foundation ranks them on economic freedom with Singapore number 1 and the US number 20.[4] In 2000, the World Health Organization ranked France at number 1 and the US at number 37 on overall health system performance.[5]

The GINI coefficient_ranks nations by wealth inequality and can be taken as a ranking of them in terms of poverty.[6] There are rankings on many categories related to poverty, health, education, social mobility, and other characteristics that several agencies track. Different ranking projects set the US in different places compared with other countries. In a 2014 comparison, the US ranked forty-fourth in health care efficiency, nineteenth in national satisfaction, and fourteenth in education.[7]

---

[2] democracymatrix.com>ranking.

[3] en.m.wikipedia.org/wiki/List_of_countries_by Human_Development.

[4] www.heritage.org/index/ranking.

[5] wikipedia.org/wiki/World_Health_Organization_ranking_of_health_systems in_2000 _#Ranking.

[6] wikipedia.org/wiki/List_of_international_rankings.

[7] rankingamerica.wordpress.com/2014/12/15/the-u-s-ranks-44th-in-health-care-efficiency/.

Those lower rankings on desirable traits and higher rankings on undesirable ones such as military spending, crime, and harming the environment do not indicate that ours is a good or true democracy. And even the better democracy at the founding of the nation has been corrupted. Three periods of corruption have occurred. Marked by economic decline, they resulted from the movement of political power from most people to a few wealthy and their private institutions. In the so-called Gilded Age, workers lost much of their income, and many lost their jobs. The recovery begun in the Franklin Roosevelt administration did not last. With the advice of the Powell memo,[8] the wealthy and their corporations took steps to undo what Roosevelt had accomplished. Beginning with the Reagan administration, wealth and power were returned more and more to corporations and to those already wealthy. At each stage of these developments, we should ask ourselves if the development came about because most American adults wanted it.

And most recently, dark money has funded politicians to gain their support for the concentration of wealth. Further corruption of democracy has been more direct as seen in the Citizens United decision, gerrymandering, superPACs, and the corruption of elected officials by making high-paying jobs in lobbying available to them when they retire if they conform to the wishes of the lobbying corporations.

Further corruption of democracy consists in the workings of the Electoral College and in the unpledged superdelegates to the Democratic national convention. There are other forces corrupting our democracy and involving voter suppression disguised as

---

[8] reclaimdemocracy.org/?s=Lewis+Powell+memo.

measures to prevent voter fraud. This latest attack on democracy is being conducted in many states, some of which have already passed state laws shortening the voting period, ending voting by mail, and enacting other means of voter suppression.

Taking David Korten's position,[9] changing the story through this work can require at least two approaches. The first is cleaning up the language of political use so that it more accurately describes the reality of American life. The second involves uncloaking the truths about the country, a process that has been started but needs more voices and more details so that the public can draw the conclusion that we must act to bring about change.[10]

First, cleaning up the language. More people need to understand how the misuse of language in politics has become a strategy of conservatives. Notice that even the term *conservative* has become soiled. In some ways, all of us can be conservative such as by working to conserve the environment, the understanding of good human relations, and the family. The use of the term has come to include the political opposition to change in our institutions, even badly needed change.

But more to the point, we need to react when the politically powerful use terms like *Democrat* or *labor* as epithets. Besides casting doubt about the intelligence and good intentions of Democrats and laborers, such usage lowers the desire of both to be known as one of them. Labor is a needed and desirable activity, honorable when carried out in a way that benefits both

---

[9] David Korten, *The Great Turning: From Empire to Earth Community*, San Francisco, Berrett-Koehler Publishing, 2006.

[10] Howard Zinn, *A People's History of the United States*, New York, HarperCollins Publishers, 1980.

self and others, and subject to improvement by the creativity of the laborer. But its association with labor unions makes it a target of disrespect even though such unions themselves are desirable and honorable. Union membership need not be a secret shame for its members. The lowering of respect for such membership has come about since the 1950s by attacks on unions by big business and their funded politicians to the point that the labor laws meant to protect unions and their members now receive less enforcement by the federal government. Union membership and its power have declined, and it has become extremely difficult to form a union. Even the small group of meatcutters at a Walmart store in Texas who joined a union in 2000 found themselves out of their jobs when the company responded by closing all its meat-cutting operations.[11]

Economic Justice for All[12] addresses the right of workers to form unions and benefit from them. It bases their formation rights on the right of association, extending their duties beyond membership to helping other workers experience fair wages and work conditions by setting and enforcing standards of justice between employers and employees.

Union locals and their higher formations such as a national union should operate democratically, allowing members to have an effective voice and vote to determine their policies and priorities. Localism, to be presented in a later chapter, has a special value in this area because of the differences in work environments among firms and localities of the same large firm. Overall policies of the

---

[11] *Washington Post*, March 4, 2000.

[12] United States Conference of Catholic Bishops, "Economic Justice for All: Catholic Social Teaching and the U.S. Economy," 1986.

national union should allow for such differences and take them into account when negotiating with the management of large firms.

The US Steelworkers union has formed a relationship with the Mondragon Corporation, a federation of worker cooperatives in the Basque region of Spain. The union leadership has learned about worker cooperatives and has decided to help bring the form into greater use in this country. The role democracy plays in co-ops shows that the union values that principle and wants to spread it among workers. It also shows the falsehood of the claim repeatedly made on the radio in the 1950s that union leadership was communist. That misuse of the term *communist* has even been applied to attempt to discredit cooperatives. More recently, far-right politicians have been applying the term *socialist* to the president and his agenda. That use as a replacement for the word *communist* may reflect the decline of its employment after the breakup of the Soviet Union. It has less power of derision because some of the most highly rated countries in Europe, mainly the Scandinavian ones, have political parties that use the term *Socialist* without shame and rely on democracy for their government formation. Unlike more-autocratic nations, their elections have the reputation of being fair and effective.

The misuse of language to reduce democracy in this country serves the aims of the powerful and wealthy, their corporations, and their owners. Other forces operate along with them to corrupt democracy in America. One of them, called dark money, refers to organizations acting as PACs of types not required to disclose their donors. They contain nonprofit organizations, for example, 501(c)(4) (social welfare), 501(c)(5) (unions), and 501(c)(6) (trade association groups.)[13] Brothers Charles and David Koch organized a network of such groups and have shown other conservatives the way to do so.

The amount of funding of election campaigns by dark money has increased greatly since its inception in the 1976 case *Buckley v. Valeo.* It has accounted for major parts of the outside spending for some candidates in their election campaigns. Because it works in secrecy, dark-money spending can be difficult to uncover for public knowledge, but some investigators have been able to identify its use in attacking political action. President Biden's recent appointment of Judge Ketanji Brown Jackson as a Supreme Court justice came under attack for supposedly being an activist judge. Support for spreading the claim came from dark money.[14] One of the most devastating features of dark money prevents its organizations from directly advocating the election of individuals but allows them to give unlimited funds to organizations that can do so.

Gerrymandering serves as another means of influencing elections by corrupting democracy. The US Census, taken every ten years, serves as the basis for defining House of Representatives districts in each state. Gerrymandering involves defining the districts in such a way that one party, usually the Republican, can have more Republican-majority districts than its opponents. The legislature, dominated by a party, draws the districts so that they concentrate the votes of their opponents into oddly shaped areas.

---

[13] wikipedia.org/wiki/Dark Money and Jane Mayer, *Dark Money: The Hidden History of the Billionaires Behind the Rise of the Radical Right*, 2016.

[14] truthout.org/articles/dark-money-is-behind-womens-groups-attacking-bidens-supreme-court-pick/.

For example, the votes of African Americans, mostly Democrats, show up in districts that include sections of multiple towns or cities linked by thinly drawn areas through rural areas. The tactic has been copied in other countries including Northern Ireland. In the US, state legislatures perform most of the redistricting while a few have nonpartisan commissions to undertake the task. Gerrymandering may favor one party by giving it more controlled districts. Even the admission of new states in the US were gerrymandered before the term was ever used. The Dakota district was divided into two states before admission of North and South Dakota so that its Republican majority would have more votes in the Senate and in the Electoral College, which chooses the president.

Created by the Constitution, the Electoral College has become the target of opposition because it continues to be used to elect presidents and vice presidents who receive a minority of the votes cast by citizens. The most recent example came in the 2016 election, when the Republican candidate, Donald Trump, was named the winner by getting 304 Electoral College votes against Clinton's 227, but his share of the votes was only 46.1 percent of the popular vote (62,984,828) while Clinton's was 48.2 percent (65,853,514).

The Electoral College remains a problem because it would be extremely difficult and expensive to advance a campaign to remove it from the Constitution. It was included in the Constitution so that states with small populations would have greater influence in the election than they would have if the outcomes were determined by just the popular vote count. For example, Wyoming would have little influence compared to New York in determining who was elected president, but in the Electoral College, Wyoming has three votes, the minimum, based on its two senators and one representative in the House of Representatives. Residents of the state have more political power in national affairs as a result of that than do residents of more-populous states.

Many holders of national offices, despite excellent retirement benefits, work to obtain jobs in lobbying firms after leaving office. Their work begins, unfortunately, while still in office, by acting according to the desires of lobbying firms. Referred to as the revolving door, it allows politicians to obtain higher paying jobs when leaving office and lobbying firms to have more access to those in office and influence in deciding policies to their clients' benefit. It represents one of the worst corruptions of democracy because it encourages officeholders to represent big business and ignore the wishes and demands of those who elected them. Like the funding of candidacies by corporations and industrial PACs, it reduces the value of the vote for those who base their choice of a candidate on qualifications and on a commitment to the common good of the district, state, or nation. It reduces the democratic influence on politics and increases the financial, autocratic control of elections and of the people.

A less serious corruption of democracy occurs in national conventions of the Democratic Party. Most delegates are pledged to support a particular individual because they are elected to do so in a party primary or caucus. But nearly 15 percent of the delegates are unpledged and thus can support any candidate. Called superdelegates, they are party leaders and elected officials. Tim Kaine, senator from Virginia and a Democrat, has tried to persuade the party to eliminate the position in conventions. In a letter to a party leader, he wrote, "I have long believed there should be no superdelegates. These positions are given undue influence in the popular nominating contest and make the process less democratic."[15] True democracy should not allow undue influence to replace the equal power of the people to decide who gets elected. This includes deciding who gets nominated.

Another corruption of democracy is practiced by political parties when they ask party members to contribute financially to candidates running for office in another state or district. It is a constant practice that reduces the influence of actual constituents. So deeply set is the practice here regarding candidates that I receive many emails from party activists and leaders asking me to contribute to candidates who will represent districts and states where I don't live. I raised the point at a meeting of a political party and asked that we consider a rule prohibiting such requests. The answer given by the chair settled the matter for the others as far as I could tell. She ended the discussion with, "You can't vote for them, but they will have an effect on your district." I failed to point out that the same argument could be raised by Russians to defend the involvement of Russia in our 2016 and 2020 presidential elections. I had become aware of the problematic character of the practice in New Mexico when I learned that the funding of the Susana Martinez campaign for governor had come mainly from outside the state. Of the $7,444,452 in contributions to her race for governor in 2010, $3,245,295 came from out of the

---

[15] www.politico.com/story/2017/11/15/tim-kaine-end-superdelegates-244944.

state;[16] $500,000 came from the national Republican governors. She later became the leader of that group.

Dark money carries on with such nonconstituent funding routinely. On the scale of their huge donations, democracy suffers corruption by it even more than by the many small donations requested and made by individuals. It shows that major parts of the political community have organized to defeat democracy and replace it with commercial autocracy. That may account for the failure of conservatives to support the investigation of the Russian interference in our national elections. It shows that we have a long way to go to develop a clear understanding of true democracy and to bring about its adoption and preservation.

To a limited extent, the word *democracy* describes the government of the US. The word *republic* also describes it. That we have a democratic republic allows the claim to be used in ways that hide its inadequacy. Even the term *republic* needs more clarity; it comes from the Latin *res*, meaning thing, and *publica*, meaning of the people. It has been translated in the idea of a republic as meaning a form of government for the common good with common rights and responsibilities of the people, a commonwealth. Praising the US for being a republic overlooks its lack of control by the people, just as applying the term *democracy* as if it were fully developed hides its limitations and domination by autocratic wealth.

In the next chapter, we will examine the true meaning of democracy as a way to explore its values and possible avenues to the improvement of ours.

---

[16] ballotpedia.org/Susana Martinez.

CHAPTER 2

The True Meaning of Democracy

The word *democracy*, which comes from the Greek words *demos*, the people, and *kratein*, to rule,[17] has multiple meanings.

1. Government by the people, either directly or through representatives; rule by the ruled.
2. A country, state, community, etc. with such a government.
3. Majority rule.
4. The acceptance and practice of the principle of equality or rights, opportunity, and treatment; lack of snobbery, as in "There is real democracy in the school."
5. The common people.
6. [D-] the Democratic Party of the United States, or the principles of this party.[18]

A search of the internet reveals many more meanings of the word. In an article on the theory of democracy, *Britannica* posted the view of John Dewey: "He also insisted that among the most important features of a social democracy should be the right of workers to participate directly in the control of the firms in which

[17] slideplayer.com/slide/10577230/.

[18] *Webster's New Universal Dictionary.*

they are employed." In this, he seemed to be an advocate of worker cooperatives.[19]

The term *democracy* describes the government of Athens while overlooking the classes of people who played no role in ruling the city. Such disagreement of the term and its application makes us wonder if those who could not participate in their government were considered to be people in the full sense of that term. But even that meaning faded when the term was adopted to refer to the nation-state. Even the people who had some of the political power of rule could not exercise it in all areas of government. It would make more sense to say that its meaning was something like a voice in some political matters. It allowed the legislators to work without necessarily responding to the wishes and demands of the larger public of citizens. That is very much the case today. Part of the problem comes from the process that must be followed to enact those wishes. If the public wants something to be reflected in law but does not act to bring it about, it may not affect the shape of laws under which they live. Time and the changes of public opinion may leave a particular political desire behind. That is not always a misfortune. Some desires arise for laws that appear desirable but would not be. For example, consider a society that wants easy access to great wealth. That desire has led to the concentration of wealth producing a large body of the impoverished and a precariat living on the edge of poverty with a life that harms family and self-development. The term "precariat" means those people who live a precarious or uncertain life. It

---

[19] "Theory of Democracy," www.britannica.com/topic/democracy/Rousseau.

creates false hope, excessive competition, excessive materialism, and domination.

Democracy has limitations. It cannot create a perfect society. It will not lift all people to a state of happiness or even satisfaction with the way society is governed. It is the best form of government, but the term is used as if it were not only the best form of government but also in full effect in the US. Suggesting that our democracy needs major improvement to make it more complete comes when some decry the need for more people to vote. But the need for far greater change to the political structure is seldom expressed. The level of democracy described by Alexis de Tocqueville in *Democracy in America*, imperfect though it was, met the definition better than it does today. Yet those who brag that America is a democracy as a way of opposing criticism often refer to de Tocqueville's presentation of it as if it were the best that could be achieved and as if it described the way we live today.

So what is the true meaning of the term *democracy*? Even recognizing that it may take various forms and involve different levels of participation, it should dominate the description of the way a society is governed for its use to be accurate. That is not the case here. Democracy as a national characteristic must be local. That is, for a nation to be called democratic, it must exercise democracy on the local level with local people deciding the rules under which they live. That would result in different rules for different parts of the country. Only rarely would a national government make a rule and only then if the variety of local rules created a major problem affecting many people. This appears to be the case. Different cities have different ordinances. Some have political offices that others don't have. And we can find such cities as a group in which the people vote to create a body of ordinances. Yet the people there live under laws made by a higher authority without their being consulted and over which they have no control. Their democracy is limited.

This introduces the concept of subsidiarity, a concept mostly unknown in the US, one I will elaborate on below. Some have become aware of the need for localism to create and maintain true democracy. That too I will elaborate on below. Notice that with all the erroneous descriptions of America as a democracy, you do not hear of your town or your state as a democracy. The point will be made that a true democratic nation must have different elements of self-rule on different levels and that the local level will have to acquire and maintain its appropriate power against higher levels.

In a truly democratic nation, citizens will have the power to participate at the local, regional, state, and national levels in a system in which the powers of each level respect the principle of subsidiarity.

Much of the news we see on TV and read in newspapers deals with political power, especially of happenings in the White House, some in Congress, and even some in a city or state. But news of the presidency dominates so much so that it appears the producers follow a rule saying that if you are to be seen as an important source of news, you must report something about the president every day even if it is just personal, something like his tripping while climbing the steps to Air Force One.[20] And report

---

[20] *New York Times*, March 19, 2021. Other newspapers covered that and other such incidents available on Wikipedia.

everything the president is known to say even when unrelated to true governing, false, or a personal attack on someone.[21]

Democracy has two major forms: direct democracy in which the people make the decisions and laws by their vote, and representative democracy in which the people elect a legislature to make its laws. In many democratic states, variations on these two forms show how general the term is today. That allows for its use to invoke many different interpretations by people. So true democracy may need to use the phrases *working democracy* to describe many nations and *deficient democracy* to describe the US as done in the democracy matrix citation from the previous chapter.

Since it has features of autocracy, that classification could also apply here. The control exercised by the wealthy and their corporations fits the definition of autocracy and violates the principle of subsidiarity. The question then arises, Have any nations adopted the principle of subsidiarity by that name? Or do some practice it without using the word for what they do in that regard? If none, it shows the true originality of the concept in the field of politics, a field in which innovations and changes have come about slowly, so we should not be surprised that it originated over a hundred years ago and has not yet taken root. Here is one of the earliest and probably most widely available sources for the meaning of subsidiarity.

> Just as it is gravely wrong to take from individuals what they can accomplish by their

[21] www.cnn.com/2018/08/18/politics/who-trump-attacks-insults-on-twitter/index.html.

> own initiative and industry and give it to the community, so also it is an injustice and at the same time a grave evil and disturbance of right order to assign to a greater and higher association what lesser and subordinate organizations can do. For every social activity ought of its very nature to furnish help (*subsidium*) to the members of the body social, and never destroy and absorb them.[22]

As the language shows, it is a moral principle, not just practical advice.

See the article on democracy by Robert A. Dahl in Britannica.com.[23] The word *devolution* suggests another precursor to subsidiarity, a topic I will present later. Wikipedia makes it clear that devolution occurs only when the central government allows it and that it is only temporary.[24] It does not mention a moral basis for devolution; maybe other sources of the term do.

Accepting the claim by Dahl and others that democracy must take the representative form for a large nation, the notion that true democracy eliminates the nation-state may cause confusion. In a world in which stronger nations seek to dominate weaker nations and in fact do, we must find other ways to end such domination than simply requiring that no true democracy can exist except in city-states. Spreading the understanding and

---

[22] Pope Pius XI, *Quadragesimo anno*, 1931, section 79.

[23] Article by Robert A. Dahl in Britannica.com, www.britannica.com/topic/democracy/The-Roman-Republic.

[24] wikipedia.org/wiki/Devolution.

practice of subsidiarity might work, but what would it do about the corporate autocracy now so widely spread?

What Are the Features of a Working Democracy?

Another claim made about the US by politicians is that this is a nation of laws, not of men or a government of laws. That expression supports the idea that our government is an institution and that it outlives the people who live under it. The twofold form of the idea echoes the use of the name of a country, sometimes referring to the people who live there or govern it and sometimes referring to it as an institution. We need to keep in mind that the US, like all nation-states, is an institution created at some point in history and has rules for its operation. We mean the Constitution, written as ours is or unwritten as is the British. Despite its tendency to persist, an institution can be dissolved. History shows examples like the Athenian democracy, the Roman Empire, the House of Hapsburg, and the Soviet Union. Because the name of a country is ambiguous, referring sometimes to the country as an institution and at other times to the people who live there (or to those who govern it, including its autocrats), we should make clear, as most partisan speech does not, which use is meant. Thus, many comments by those in office aim to persuade a broader public by calling to mind the institutional framework and its characteristics even when those characteristics have long been neglected or failed to exist. The "liberty and justice for all" in the American Pledge of Allegiance expresses a hope, not a reality. The term *indivisible* shares that fate since the nation can be divided, broken up into other institutions, and divided in its partisan politics as the US currently is.

Democracy may describe an institution more or less accurately, so the ranking of nations by their democracies makes sense. The more accurate application of the terms *democracy* or *democratic* appears when used to refer to small groups. One of the most democratic is the worker cooperative firm. It practices control with one vote per person and majority rule. Another institution, cohousing, bases some of its group decisions on consensus. Since such institutions in California have homeowner associations, the law governing them mandates that a board of directors govern, and the board makes decisions democratically by majority rule instead of by consensus. And while the owners elect the board, an act of democracy, they do not vote on policies by majority rule.

The fundamental idea of democracy, rule by the people, has such strong appeal that the term ends up being applied to nations and other institutions when its application is false. Even the names of countries such as the Democratic Republic of Vietnam, the Democratic Republic of the Congo, or the Central African Republic indicate a desire to be seen as democratic when democracy doesn't strongly characterize their governments. Each of the named countries is indexed as a moderate autocracy in the ranking by the University of Wurzburg "Ranking of Countries by Quality of Democracy."[25] It applies three dimensions—freedom, equality, and control—to five institutional characteristics, procedures of decision, regulation of the intermediate sphere, public communication, guarantee of rights, and rules settlement and implementation.

---

[25] democracymatrix.com/ranking.

The terms for indexing the nations show that democracy and autocracy do not constitute the only possibilities. The greater number of descriptions, there called classifications, shows that democracy is not an all-or-nothing principle when applied and exercised. With its classification of deficient democracy, the US would not fit the meaning of true democracy as a working democracy. And even those classified that way have less than perfect characteristics in the three dimensions. Denmark, ranked number 1, has a total value index of 0.958, not 1.0. And the US has a total value index of 0.811. While the goal should be to reach an index of 1.0, getting as close to it as possible would do much to enhance the lives of people living in a nation. We must keep in mind that the degree to which a nation is democratic is not the only basis for determining the quality of life in a nation, but it is one of the most important. Economic, social, artistic, and environmental attributes affect us as individuals and families. A higher index of democracy should give us the power to influence those others, but we still must recognize that much depends not on government but on our decisions and actions as individuals acting for ourselves and for others, sometimes alone and sometimes with others. We must find balance between what we desire for ourselves and what should rightly belong to collective decision-making. Pure individualism will encourage us to act as tyrants while complete acceptance of all collective decisions will render us passive and ineffective.

David Korten and Chalmers Johnson present imperialism as the major problem of civilization. For both, it threatens the very existence of its practitioners. For Korten, it even threatens humanity with extinction because it has led to environmental destruction that wipes out the natural resources needed for human life. The subtitle of Johnson's book *Nemesis* is *The Last Days of the American Republic.* He wrote another book decrying the horrors of imperialism: *The Sorrows of Empire.* Much of Korten's work *The Great Turning: From Empire to Earth Community* explores the problems of the immature stage of consciousness named the imperial. I will summarize the five levels of consciousness he discussed since they are an important part of his book.[26]

The first order of consciousness, named magical, is that of children between the ages of two and six, a period during which they cannot recognize the consequences of their actions but see all events as if they were the product of magic. The second order, the imperial, begins to develop around the age six and comes to full development in the teen years and usually lasts until about age thirty. It is marked by an awareness of consequences but a lack of understanding of justice, personal responsibility, and acting on a personalized ethical code. It concerns Korten more than the others because those who reach that stage may fail to move to the next, around age thirty, and continue to see the world as a place where they need not concern themselves with the needs of others except when they can bargain to get something they want in return. Many people fail to advance to the next and more beneficial stage of social consciousness. That order can begin in the teen years and fully develop in the thirties and reach the point that its subject sees justice more broadly but limited to the group that the individual feels membership in. After that, cultural consciousness develops and sees the importance of justice for all, not just for oneself or one's group. The fifth order, spiritual

---

[26] *The Great Turning*, 43–48.

consciousness, supports a view of a world in which all creation has value and in which all people have dignity and deserve justice. Those who reach that order engage in the cocreation of the world.

It raises the question whether a nation of people with too many adults remaining in the imperial stage of consciousness tends to support and demand imperialism as a political position. Korten implies that the connection accounts for US imperialism. He considers the solution of the problem not to involve simple opposition to political imperialism but changing the story by which people learn to adopt desirable political values. While not mentioning imperialism, *Economic Justice for All* sees the connection between economic justice and democracy on all levels as well as their mutual reinforcement.[27] It points out also that the development of democracy has been an experiment, one that is not complete and that must be continued. That it has taken various forms in different nations and over time in some of them gives us the basis for studying how effectively different features of the variations have contributed to a sustainable good life for humans and their institutions. Since being experimental is part of the meaning of democracy, we cannot predict a time when the experiment will be complete and democracy will harden into an unchanging set of characteristics or values. But some of its characteristics and values should persist throughout the experiment. What are those characteristics and values?

Wikipedia names the cornerstones of democracy as including freedom of assembly and speech, inclusiveness and equality,

---

[27] See *Economic Justice for All: Catholic Social Teaching and the U.S. Economy in Origins*, NC documentary services and www.usccb.org/upload/economic_justice_for_all.pdf.

membership, consent, voting, right to life, and minority rights.[28] Other listings of the values sound like a list from the American political powers because the list includes language from our Constitution for some of the values. That full list includes life, liberty, the pursuit of happiness, justice, equality, diversity, truth, popular sovereignty, patriotism, and the rule of law. Wikipedia indicates that there is no consensus about the meaning of the term and refers to one work that tells us that there are 2,234 descriptions of democracy.[29] Another theory requires three fundamental principles: upward control (sovereignty residing on the lowest levels of authority), political equality, and acceptable institutions.[30] When presented as an ethical principle, upward control may be taken as another name for subsidiarity.

With so many different sets of values or principles for defining democracy, what meaning can we apply to the term? Korten uses the expression "deep democracy" instead of true democracy. A search for the word *democracy* in his book on Kindle produced ninety-three pages of his use of the term, each with two references.[31] Since his goal is promoting earth community, the basic role of democracy there must involve supporting it and making it possible. It makes clearer what he means by earth community. I think he means a form of global association of people that is as strong, beneficial, and stable as local community

---

[28] wikipedia.org/wiki/Democracy.

[29] Ibid.

[30] "On Democracy 1" by Richard Kimber, University of Keele, UK, 1989 article in *Scandinavian Political Studies*, tidsskrift.dk/scandinavian_political_studies/article/view/32645/30739.

[31] David Korten, *The Great Turning*, San Francisco, Berrett-Koehler Publishers, Inc. 2006.

can be under true or deep democracy even though it lacks the interpersonal relations of small community.

Richard Kimber's article "On Democracy" insists that determining what constitutes democracy involves qualitative rather than quantitative considerations. Where many of the definitions rely on polls for making the determination, he looks at the working of government to decide. His requirement of upward control has a source different from that of subsidiarity. Where subsidiarity makes a moral claim for leaving many matters in the hands of more local levels of decision-making, government, upward control makes no moral claim but one of description.

Another document can help us understand the meaning of democracy. The Earth Charter "is an international declaration of fundamental values and principles considered useful by its supporters for building a just, sustainable, and peaceful global society in the 21st century."[32] It took six years (1994–2000) to draft the document and reach a wide consensus on its contents among representatives of many nations. Its only critics have been ultraconservatives claiming it is secular and espouses socialism. While it presents its actions as ethical obligations, it leaves them open to adoption by any religious group and espouses principles not found in national socialism. Its thirteenth main principle is, "Strengthen democratic institutions at all levels, and provide transparency and accountability in governance, inclusive participation in decision-making, and access to justice." The supporting principles include three that appears to support

---

[32] For an online copy of Earth Charter, see earthcharter.org/library/the-earth-charter-text/.

subsidiarity without mentioning the word "subsidiarity" or the adoption of it.

> a. Uphold the right of everyone to receive clear and timely information on environmental matters and all development plans and activities which are likely to affect them or in which they have an interest.
>
> b. Support local, regional and global civil society, and promote the meaningful participation of all interested individuals and organizations in decision making.
>
> f. Strengthen local communities, enabling them to care for their environments, and assign environmental responsibilities to the levels of government where they can be carried out most effectively.

Subsidiarity and localism find support in the document without being named. The document, in addition to being a carefully considered and developed set of statements on the topic of environmental conservation, provides a way to the future. Reading it creates a sense of inspiration from its first words in the preamble and its concluding words in "The Way Forward." One would do well to read it regularly and to use it in the education of the young and the organization of needed social changes.

Further Thoughts on the True Meaning of Democracy

One meaning of democracy describes it as direct, in which the people make the rules, and representative, in which elected officials do so. Because our Constitution provides for the election of representatives, I will include that feature in the meaning of the term here. And because of our features of referendum, initiative, and recall, it involves direct democracy as well. Because we have a federal government and its laws and offices and state and local governments with their laws and offices, we could say that the US has four levels of government, each of which has elements of direct and representative democracy. And because the instances of the lower levels of government are so many, their variety of laws and details of representation prevent us from a simple description of democracy on each level.

We need not describe all the variations to deal with the other two themes of the book—subsidiarity and localism—that allow for such variation. Just to mention one level, the many cities or local communities have such different economies, population sizes, health conditions, food sources, demographics, educational resources, climates, natural resources, and physical structure to name just a few differences that one set of rules for all of them simply would not work. California, one example, shows enormous variety at all three levels—state, county, and community. It has a population greater than many countries and an economy of concentrated wealth with a few examples of distributed wealth in its worker cooperatives. Its coastal climate differs from its internal climate, thus requiring variety in its rules.

One example of how climate and natural resources have

produced ordinances can be seen in California, where the cutting down of an oak tree is prohibited without authorization by city councils. Its cities have different rules for applying the law including the size of the property, the variety of oak tree, and the thickness of its trunk. El Paso de Robles, meaning the Pass of Oaks, was named by those who noticed its large number of oaks and its location between mountain ranges. Its rule reflects the desire that the name of the city not become meaningless as it would if all such trees were destroyed. While that may not be the motive for the state law, it still makes sense locally.

With all its variety of laws and the means of making them, we accept then a meaning of democracy that bases political power in a describable population living in a particular area, the meaning of direct democracy. We also accept representative democracy, the placing of political power in larger institutions but only when needed in situations where the local people and their rule cannot achieve the common good.

The multiplicity of governing bodies in the US does not excuse the use of the word *democracy* to promote the belief that America's government is the best in the world and should not be criticized. The problems caused by the widespread corruption in government and the concentration of power in the hands of the wealthy and corporations show that our government does not fit the full meaning of true democracy. While some use the term in the context of recommending the form and its fuller development, others use it to excuse policies that reduce its benefits for large portions of the population. The most frequent application of the term by conservatives appears to help put many Americans into a state of passivity. By exaggerating the good of the country, they lull many to a political sleep even to the point that it reduces voter turnout, especially among those who would otherwise want to see more-progressive policies. Combined with the spread of state laws creating voter suppression, it helps solidify domination by the wealthy.

The goal, then, would not convert the national level into the sort of democracy that could be achieved on the local level, but it would prevent the national government officials and their departments from stripping the true democracy from local cities and local regions. It would change the description of the US from deficient democracy to working democracy, making the use of the term in describing the nation less of a smoke screen and more of a true description.

In the next chapter, we will explore some of the consequences of our failure to progress as a true democracy.

CHAPTER 3

The Consequences of the Lack of True Democracy

The nations with lower positions on the democracy index pose problems for their citizens and for other nations. Those problems tend to reinforce one another. Less democracy contributes to the concentration of wealth, which contributes to the concentration of power, which tends to reduce the quality of democracy. The poor tend to fail to exercise their political rights, to vote less, and to find getting to the polls more difficult. This occurs in the US as a form of racial discrimination, which is increasing in many states.

The citizens of a more truly democratic nation would have a higher level of participation in it. That would give them the power to see that the economic system permits more of them to share the wealth that they produce through their work on a level that lifts the poor out of poverty and prevents those above the poverty line from falling into poverty. That group has come to be known as the precariat, workers who are close to falling into poverty. A true democracy would have no precariat, a group rendered obedient to those who dominate without the right to do so. The social, economic, and political effects on citizens of deficient democracies have reached the point that even the controlled media can no longer avoid the subject and are reporting on it daily.

Another effect, environmental destruction, has become so serious that the media report on it, but rarely do they make the connection between it and the concentration of power in business corporations. As an exception to that, they do report the position of the oil and gas industry in its opposition to a politically organized movement to stop the extraction and use of natural resources to create energy. Those industries even oppose proposals to increase the use of large-scale solar and wind energy capture, often doing so by pointing out the minor problems of those means.[33]

So serious is the problem of environmental neglect that some have pointed out that its continuation threatens the destruction of human society. We know already that many species of wild animals and plants face the risk of extinction caused by human environmental impact. The knowledge that it also creates the threat of human extinction has yet to appear in the popular media even if they know about it.

The political argument on the topic centers on global warming. Scientific evidence along with changing weather patterns and climates shows that it is occurring. Yet those who serve the desires of concentrated wealth, beyond neglecting the environment, claim that global warming is not happening and go further by claiming that the scientists are simply wrong. If we are seeing climate change, they say that it is a normal event that has occurred many times in the past without any human cause or connection to pollution.

In a more democratic society, the concern about global

---

[33] A search of the internet reveals many sources condemning the use of wind and solar as energy sources. But they fail to point out how known hazards, such as injury to birds by flying into wind generators, could be mitigated. And for the claim that solar energy devices use hazardous chemicals, we need to recognize the continuing improvement of them as they develop. They also fail to consider the reduction of environmental damage that renewable energy sources promote.

warming, climate change, and the threat of extinction has greater recognition even if not complete consensus. That greater recognition leads citizens to demand environmental protection involving support for carbon-free power production and a limit on the extraction and mining of carbon-based energy sources. That the long history of our planet includes climate changes does not excuse us from avoiding being the cause of another one. Our obligations to global life and human beings need to be kept in mind and stand as values we protect.

Less democratic nations have a higher incidence of violence among their citizens.[34] Violence creates fear, an important tool for the domination of a society by the rich and powerful. It has been used to justify racism, an excessive application of taxes to militarism, and the perpetuation of income inequality. It destroys trust between people of different races and encourages isolation and segregation. The high level of military spending reduces trust between nations. How much of the US budget goes to military spending on weapons production, transportation, storage, maintenance, training for their use, and on the deployment of military in the many US bases and in other countries? It uses 15 percent of federal spending on so-called defense and half of discretionary spending. It spends more than the next ten highest spending countries combined—China, India, Russia, Saudi Arabia, France, Germany, United Kingdom, Japan, South Korea, and Brazil. It maintains nearly 800 bases in seventy foreign countries and territories; there are no foreign military bases in the

---

[34] Eric Neumayer, "Good Policy Can Lower Violent Crime: Evidence from a Cross-National Panel of Homicide Rates, 1980–97." *Journal of Peace Research* 40, no. 6 (2003): 619–40, http://www.jstor.org/stable/3648380.

US. Approximately 165,000 of its military forces are stationed outside the US. With over 1 million active-duty members in six branches, it is the third largest with China and India ahead. The full military size includes reservists and should also include the number of civilians working in military departments and bases. Except for civilians working in the US Army (more than 330,000), a total number that would include US civilians serving domestically and overseas is hard to find.

What can justify having so much of its budget and so many of its citizens involved in military spending and work? Secretary of Defense Lloyd J. Austin III said,

> As the Secretary of Defense, my chief priority is defending America from enemies foreign and domestic and ensuring our troops remain the world's preeminent fighting force … The budget provides us the mix of capabilities we need most and stays true to our focus on the pacing challenge from the People's Republic of China, combating the damaging effects of climate change on our military installations, and modernizing our capabilities to meet the advanced threats of tomorrow. Importantly, this budget invests in our people, the brave women and men in uniform around the world who serve on behalf of this great nation.[35]

[35] Statement by Secretary of Defense Lloyd J. Austin III on the President's Fiscal Year 2022 Budget. www.defense.gov/News/Releases/Release/Article/2638711/the-department-of-defense-releases-the-presidents-fiscal-year-2022-defense-budg/.

Contrary to the advice of presidents George Washington and Dwight D. Eisenhower, our government and political pundits continue to encourage the belief that we must have foreign allies and adversaries on a long-term basis and that the military-industrial complex serves freedom and our safety. They even use the word *dominance* as if it were a proper goal for foreign policy and to justify continuing interference in and even invading other countries to maintain it. The belief that the wealthiest nation in the world should use so much of its resources to impose its will on the rest of the world and to try to shape other countries' internal and foreign policies has kept us engaged in wars for so many years.[36] Besides taking so many of our citizens from their families and communities, where they could work to produce benefits for themselves, their families, and the community, it has also increased the nation's deficit to the point that it can no longer adequately maintain its infrastructure.

In a later chapter, I will present the topic of subsidiarity and the immoral interference by a more central government into less central ones when not needed. We need a term for the immoral practice of a single nation attempting to control the rest of the world. Perhaps *imperialism* best describes it. The costs of imperialism are high for the dominated nations and for the dominating nation. We have lost prosperity for a large part of our population. We should notice that our behavior toward other countries has caused many of them to increase their militarization

---

[36] While the number of years changes as time passes, this report in 2020 shows a long history. The US has been at war for 225 out of 243 years since 1776, www.thenews.com.pk/print/595752-the-us-has-been-at-war-225-out-of-243-years-since-1776.

at the cost of their citizens. The excuse that they pose a threat to us displays great hypocrisy since our militaristic behavior poses a threat to them.

A nation that fails to practice subsidiarity at home and engages in international imperialism at the same time needs fundamental changes to justify its existence as a political unit. Even that is threatened as the world comes to see the human costs such a state imposes. At the peak of their geographic size, eighteenth-century England and the twentieth-century Soviet Union provide two examples. Currently, the UK may have to face what its predecessor had to deal with as its control of Northern Ireland still raises conflict and questions of its right to dominate it. Other examples include Russia's domination of its neighbors Crimea and Ukraine and China's domination of Taiwan.

Both of those policies—imperialism and wrongful subordination—prevent the practice of true democracy, especially when practiced together. Those practices were obvious during the time of powerful monarchies. Monarchs dominated their communities and citizens, and some engaged in imperialism, a fact well known to Americans as the reason for the American Revolution. Having successfully opposed monarchy, we now have a government that has failed to create the democracy it praised as monarchy's replacement. Unfortunately, the rise of industrialism took power away from the people and gave it to the few.

The militarism of the US has grown with the development of weapons. The manufacturers take a large portion of the federal budget and act to influence the government to maintain their income. By spreading their facilities throughout the country, they make the point that jobs in many states depend on protecting the industry. That argument, made not to the general public but to the officials elected there to control national policy, has succeeded in sustaining the flow of money to them. In a true democracy, the people would choose policies that reduced the risks and costs created by excessive military development. They would demand foreign policies that sought peace between nations based on mutual good treatment and the trust it creates. They would demand federal observation of subsidiarity and local control of matters within the capability of states, counties, and cities.

If the Enlightenment has a lasting meaning to Americans, it must reside in its continued exploration of democracy with experimentation and the results of that made known to all society and its worth considered. Our current nation lacks transparency because the ruling forces reject it, needing to disguise their motives and the very conditions their autocracy has created.

Even human employment suffers. Much of the justification that conservatives offer for the economic policies they support maintains that they create jobs. We even speak of employment as having a job. But strictly speaking, workers do not *have* jobs; employers have them and can create or terminate them at will. If employees truly had jobs, that would allow them greater control of their conditions and a better return to the employees of the wealth created by their work; workers would have more bargaining power with their employers.

The lack of a working democracy has practically destroyed the association of workers into unions, weakening them to the point that large corporations can prevent them from being formed. The number of American unions in private firms have declined since the 1950s. Formerly, over 30 percent of workers were members;

now it is about 10 percent.[37] The representation of unions by secondary organizations is rarely if ever heard of today. In the fifties, their policies and actions were often in the news. The name was so denigrated over time that it hardly appears. The AFL-CIO still exists but is rarely mentioned in public media.

Another effect of declining democracy shows up in education. Years ago, we were taught that our leaders had responsibility for informing the public of those subjects related to the exercise of democracy, the values to guide us, the effects of policy, and the facts on which they were based. But today, rather than informing us, our politicians go to great lengths to misinform us about such matters. The previous presidential administration gained its support in part by that practice but even more by exaggerated partisanship. In the news we hear now, what matters most is not the effect of political decisions by people in office on the welfare of the nation's citizens but on their effect on a political party's chances of dominating. A misinformed public will tolerate imperialism even when the destructiveness of its history has been documented over and over. Now, the effect on the few who rule matters more to journalists than the effect on the whole nation to say nothing of the effects on foreign populations.

"Central Intelligence Agency: The President's Private Army" is the title of a chapter in Chalmers Johnson's book *Nemesis*, on the creation and corruption of the CIA. It tells how the agency changed from an investigative agency to one that has committed assassinations, bribed foreign nations, intervened in the overthrow of foreign governments, and behaved to help keep the president's

---

[37] "Labor Unions in the United States," wikipedia.org/wiki/Labor_unions_in_the_United_States#History.

violations of law and the Constitution from becoming known by the public. It has done a lot to create hostility toward the US in Latin America, the Far East, and in Iraq and Afghanistan.

One of its most noted and condemned adventures involved the overthrow of Salvador Allende, president of Chile, leader of a democratic and peaceful nation, replacing him with a cruel and dishonest General Augusto Pinochet. It also tells of the horrors of CIA involvement in Pakistan, Afghanistan, and Iraq with the aid of Saudi Arabia and the United Arab Republic. It is still ongoing. Its covert operations, including so-called renditions, have become a major source of anti-American feeling and policy overseas. It has totally given up acting as an information source for the president according to Johnson.

On further reading of *Nemesis*, one learns just how much US effort and money go into the fine-tuning of our overseas military empire. Especially in the Middle East, the opening and closing of bases and the changes in agreements about their locations and operations have taken up a lot of time for its management. I learned that in some places, the local nation pays the US to station its military there, slightly reducing the US cost of maintaining its foreign occupation, but we do not learn to what degree that is.

Most striking is the justification for this situation being offered—to protect the US and its interests from terrorists. The reality has more to do with our access to their rich supplies of petroleum. The desire for cheap oil to keep our cars and trucks running for the benefit of big oil ends up affecting our foreign policy, backs US imperialism, and creates pollution, increases global warming, and damages the environment.

The cure for this situation and the waste it involves must come from growing democracy at home along with greater knowledge of military costs and the immorality of what we have been doing. It will not change by more democracy alone while Americans tolerate it to gain jobs and income.

Another lesson we must learn is that if some believe our economy requires excessive militarization to produce enough jobs, we need to change that so that other, more-supportive work can occupy people currently involved in wasteful and harmful military occupations. We should not be dependent on imperialism as an economic strategy.

We will see in other chapters that other ways of producing economic benefits for all are available. They would end much of the killing and destruction of war and the hostility that accompanies intervention. They would promote peace and stability and family and community prosperity.

CHAPTER 4

A Challenge to the Status Quo

If we are to prevent the collapse of the US and the further suffering and impoverishment of its people, we must act to change the direction we are headed.

A growing literature has begun to provide the factual base we need to understand how to act. In his master work, *The Great Turning: From Empire to Earth Community*, David Korten sees the problem in what he calls the story. We must change the story being told to generations because it is untrue. It tells about a nation that practices autocracy while many of its leaders claim that it is the world's greatest democracy. Our politicians have used the story to try to justify imperialism and the concentration of wealth and power while ignoring the many who suffer poverty, ill health, and stressful, uncertain lives. They present international relations as a contest in which we must struggle to be the strongest and the wealthiest nation. It presents competition as the natural way of relating among nations, a competition we must win to prevent any rogue state from coming to dominate us. From this, it follows that we must have the strongest military in the world and that it must be seen as such by all nations. From that, it follows that we spend more than the next ten highest spending nations combined on military personnel, weapons, weapon development, and the support needed to base our military in over eighty other countries while allowing none to base theirs here. We divide the world into friends and foes, allies and adversaries, keeping the flow of stories going, especially about the adversaries daily before the American people.

The locus of the stories has changed over time and now concerns the Middle East, China, and North Korea with the development of nuclear weapons among those nations serving to produce the fear needed to justify our enormous military budget. When negotiation with any of them aims at getting them to stop building nuclear weapons and delivery systems, it never includes the reciprocity of the US getting rid of its nuclear weapons. The lack of mutuality in the relationships motivates the others to continue their military policies while making them look stubborn and self-centered. Such hypocrisy on our part needs greater exposure as a part of changing the story. But we are told that our military behavior regarding our adversaries has behind it the motive of protecting the freedom Americans supposedly enjoy.

Some Americans attempt to counter that version of the American story. Ralph Nader has spent many years exposing the falsehood of the story and its use to maintain the domination and wealth of the few over the many. He exposed the way the wealthy have gone about choosing who will run for national office and how they have paid for the campaigns for their elections. They have used their wealth to bring formerly diverse and locally owned news outlets under their control through their purchase by national media companies. Those companies control the editorial policy that at one time reflected local values very different from those currently presented. It has helped to shape the thinking of many Americans in ways that support militarism and imperialism.

Yet on many issues, as Nader pointed out, the truth has

managed to leak through to many and to create a situation in which the desires of most citizens for many changes to policy play no role in shaping national policy. He has pointed out at least twenty-five major issues on which the partisan divide should fail to stand in the way because they are issues on which both Democrats and Republicans on the ground level agree.[38] But their agreement has no effect because political leaders answer not to their constituencies but to their funders, the individuals, corporations, and PACs who fund their campaigns and occupy offices in Washington as the shadow government.

When the use of their money to control government begins to affect public opinion against their control in a visible way, they turn to dark money as the answer. That means that the wealthy form financial relations with others whose identity is kept secret so that their donations and ensuing control of politicians will remain unknown to the general public. The book by that name should be widely read and understood as it shows the dependence on a form of corporation that allows such organizations to form and avoid paying taxes as 501(c)(4) entities.[39]

---

[38] In many interviews, Nader has pointed out that there are at least twenty-five political goals on which there is bipartisan agreement among large numbers of American citizens. See his books *Unstoppable: The Emerging Left–Right Alliance to Dismantle the Corporate State*, 2015, and *Breaking Through Power: It's Easier Than We Think*, 2016.

[39] Jane Mayer Dark Money: *The Hidden History of the Billionaires Behind the Rise of the Radical Right*, Doubleday, 2016.

Changing the Story with Social Teaching

Another source of the call for changing the story comes from Catholic social teaching. Beginning with Pope Leo XIII's 1891 encyclical Rerum novarum, On *the Condition of Workers*,[40] the church has attempted to teach that the dominant economic and social practices affecting societies, individuals, and families should support them instead of holding them in poverty while the few wealthy take much more than they need or deserve. It reviewed the relations between the working classes and the owning classes and condemned the misery and suffering they cause and perpetuate for the poor. It lays down the actions needed to meet the moral requirements for justice in economic relations between the two by asserting the right of workers to form unions and to engage in fair and just negotiations for living wages and benefits needed by their families to lift and keep them out of poverty.

While addressing the bishops, clergy, and faithful of the church in terms of their religious heritage, *Rerum novarum* also presents the reasonable and natural basis for its proposals, which those of other faiths can adopt. It describes the level of material wealth needed for a good life as an adequate level, denying that great wealth adds to the happiness of its possessors. That claim has been shown to be true over the years; excessive wealth in some cases causes an excess of pleasure seeking that leads to misery. But the focus on the working classes, their needs, and their rights to have those needs satisfied sets out a landscape of social and economic justice for correcting the misery of many at the time it was written and for all generations following.

---

[40] *Rerum novarum* is at www.papalencyclicals.net/leo13/l13rerum.htm.

It also describes the political structure of its time in a way that others would further develop later. It presents one of the major topics of this work: subsidiarity. Section 32 describes the meaning of the state and mentions its need to avoid "being open to the suspicion of undue interference," one description of the lack of subsidiarity.[41] See also sections 53 and 54. Section 11 mentions the priority of the family over the state because of its being natural and much older. Section 13 elaborates on that, and section 14 tells why the authority of the family must not be overridden by the state. This criticism of socialism in centralizing too much authority suggests to me that our autocratic state does that also but it is not mentioned in our society. We are like the communist states in that regard. Section 16 mentions one way the condition of working people can improve: "Recourse should be had, in due measure and degree, to the intervention of the law and of State authority." Section 45 mentions "undue interference on the part of the State." Section 47 preserves the right of private property against the state.

It stresses the requirement that we look at the needs of all the people and the way government contributes to providing for those needs. A government that serves mainly the wishes of those whose needs are already met at the expense of those whose wishes and needs are not met should change its practices. That part of the encyclical is timely today because the situation of the Gilded Age that motivated its writing obtains again today. The concentration of wealth is much higher than it was then, and the number of the poor much greater. So missing are we of the values of distributive justice that we apply charity as if it had a permanent object, that

---

41 Ibid.

the poor would always be poor and as if nothing could be done by those with higher incomes and wealth to alter the condition of the poor except temporarily. Fortunately, forms of charity other than giving money are beginning to show the possibility of long-term improvement of the lives of recipients.[42] But as with some of the other themes of Catholic social teaching, the word has not spread widely enough to make it an effective influence on individual, corporate, and national action.

Pope Pius XI picked up the theme again in 1931 in his encyclical *Quadragesimo anno, Forty Years.*[43] Its English title is *On Reconstruction of the Social Order.* It stresses the need for other changes to the morals of social and economic organization. He rejects classical liberalism and its support of individualism and opposes socialism and its support of collectivism. He encourages cooperation without direct reference to worker cooperatives. By doing so and by praising the development of many new forms of social organization being created by associated persons in many fields, he could be understood as a supporter of cooperatives.

While not reaching the point of naming and supporting worker cooperatives, the encyclical recognizes the change and development of theory about socialism. Having seen that it led to Communism, a form of social, economic, and political organization he strongly opposed, he recognized further development of socialism and supported allowing for some private

[42] A book by Mauricio Miller led to the creation of an organization, Family Independence Initiative, to help the poor organize themselves in a way that lifts them out of poverty. See *The Alternative: Most of What You Believe about Poverty Is Wrong*, Lulu Publishing Services, 2017.

[43] *Quadragesimo anno*, www.papalencyclicals.net/pius11/p11quadr.htm.

property while retaining government control of some kinds of property "that carry with them a dominating power so great that cannot without danger to the general welfare be entrusted to private individuals."[44] But he still opposed it on religious grounds "if it remains truly Socialism" because he saw it then as occupied only with material needs and supporting materialism.

Further development up to this time has altered that again. Many see socialism as primarily the government providing a society's needs; it leaves space for private or group ownership of the means of production. Another meaning advocates for the public ownership of a few forms of businesses—electrical utilities, water supply, public transportation, and part of public media. So rather than reject Pope Pius's condemnation of all the influences of socialism, we take the position that what is learned from it and some of its current and hoped-for developments shine a light on the moral base upholding it: justice and concern for all people.

While not using the term *socialism* at all, *Economic Justice for All* reflects the change of attitude toward its meaning.[45] It mentions the assertion of Pope John Paul II that "One cannot exclude the socialization, in suitable conditions, of certain means of production" citing *Laborem exercens* (*On Human Work*).[46] In its early pages, that work recalls other works by church leaders on the topic and its change from the focus on justice within a country to world economic justice and its need to deal with the poverty and suffering of entire populations of some countries.

---

[44] Ibid., section 114.

[45] *Economic Justice for All*, section 115.

[46] *Laborem exercens*, section 14, www.vatican.va/content/john-paul-ii/en/encyclicals/documents/hf_jp-ii_enc_14091981_laborem-exercens.html.

It refers to Pope John XXIII's encyclicals *Pacem in terris*[47] and *Mater et magistra*.[48] These influenced the work of the Second Vatican Council and its doctrine on the relation of peace and justice as well as the encyclical *Populorum progressio*[49] by Pope Paul VI. Overall, they consider the change in work brought about by advances in technology and other aspects of economics.

Laborem exercens brings up the topic of solidarity, the basis of cooperatives, as an historical development in reaction to the industrialization with its concentration of wealth, modification of work, and the loss of freedom and support it caused workers. Overall, the encyclical stresses the spiritual aspect of work and the way it reflects how humanity was created in the image of God. It sees in work not simply a means to obtain wealth but also to share in the creation of the world.

Pacem in terris also discusses subsidiarity, referring to it by that name. It applies it to the public authority of "the world community" in its effort to solve the problems that the nations have not been able to solve for better relations. Like its application on the state level, it prohibits limiting the power of the states or arrogating their functions to itself. It repeats four requirements for obtaining peace—truth, justice, charity, and freedom.

Economic Justice for All focuses on justice for the poor. "Decisions must be judged in light of what they to do for the

---

47 www.vatican.va/content/john-xxiii/en/encyclicals/documents/hf_j-xxiii_enc_11041963_pacem.html.

48 www.vatican.va/content/john-xxiii/en/encyclicals/documents/hf_j-xxiii_enc_15051961_mater.html.

49 www.vatican.va/content/paul-vi/en/encyclicals/documents/hf_p-vi_enc_26031967_populorum.html.

poor, what they do to the poor, and what they enable the poor to do for themselves."[50]

It addresses four subjects: "1) employment, 2) poverty, 3) food and agriculture, and 4) the U.S. role in the global economy."[51]

It recommends balance and moderation in attempting to help poor people. "Paternalistic programs which do too much for and too little with the poor are to be avoided."[52]

It develops this advice further.

> Poor people must be empowered to take charge of their own futures and become responsible for their own economic advancement. Personal motivation and initiative, combined with social reform, are necessary elements to assist individuals in escaping poverty. By taking advantage of opportunities for education, employment, and training, and by working together for change, the poor can help themselves to be full participants in our economic, social, and political life.[53]

It recommends other means for fostering self-help among the poor including worker cooperatives.[54] This topic will be discussed further in this chapter.

---

[50] Chap. 1, section 24. Enabling the poor "to do for themselves" became the guiding principle for the Family Independence Initiative or FII, a topic to be discussed here later.

[51] Chap. 3, section 133.

[52] Chap. 3, section 188.

[53] Chap. 3, section 201.

[54] Chap. 3, section 200.

The Family Independence Initiative, now named UpTogether, has continued to grow. It has members in fifty states and Puerto Rico. It makes donations to groups of families organizing to get themselves out of poverty. Its major aid is not financial but the encouragement of initiative in forming and using local organizations, guiding the poor to find out how others have gotten out of poverty, and what those in their group are able to do to advance that goal. It has many success stories. A major one concerns the story of Ted Ngoy. After fleeing Cambodia under Pol Pot and settling in California, he took a job at a Winchell's donut shop, became a franchise owner, and ended up starting his own donut business. As other Cambodian refugees came to California, he helped them start their own donut shop businesses. Now, most California donut shops are owned by people from Cambodia. The Winchell's I ran in the late sixties is gone, and many former Winchell's are now Donut King shops, named after Ngoy's nickname.

Beyond writings influencing our understanding of the problems of concentrated wealth and power, some Americans have turned to action to bring the issues to the public's attention and to gain support for reform. One major US event, Occupy Wall Street, in September 2011 in Zuccotti Park in New York, caught national attention and spread the word about "social and economic inequality, greed, corruption and the undue influence of corporations on government—particularly the financial services sector."[55] The group of protesters, using the motto "We are the 99 percent," chose direct action over petitioning authorities as the way to bring about change.

---

[55] en.wikipedia.org/wiki/Occupy_Wall_Street.

Occupy Wall Street was initiated by a Canadian, Kalle Lasn, in his anticonsumerist magazine *Adbusters*. A February 2011 magazine article in it featured an image of a dancer on top of the Wall Street statue of a charging bull while recommending the protest begin on September 17. The action was imitated in many places against major banks and other mega businesses.

I attended a meeting of an organization in Albuquerque, New Mexico, that was formed as the result of an Occupy Albuquerque group formed there. While the movement has faded under that name, its influence has continued to engage many citizens in the effort to reject consumerism and the other aspects of our anti-democratic commercialism and inequality. It is a growing movement meant to simplify personal life, an action to be undertaken by individuals rather than the government. It has caught on with many people, some of whom willingly share information about what they have done to live simple lives. Some even refer to it as minimalism.

Did Occupy Wall Street fail? Now that it is no longer occupying and has no permanent organization or website, some claim that it has failed. It did not lead during its heyday to legislation supporting its values, and it did not pass the baton to the next generation to go on using its methods. Yet it made headlines, was imitated in many US cities, and influenced the Democratic Party to begin recognizing progressive leaders such as Bernie Sanders. That part of the movement is not dead despite the rise of Republican action to suppress voting by the poor and overworked racial minorities in the country.

While recent support by the Supreme Court of state voter-suppression laws adds to the fear that the failure is real and permanent, those actions may cause the left to rise again, organize, and act to overcome what is happening now to further strengthen democracy and to increase the participation it needs. When Americans recognize that political participation is both a right and a duty, voter turnout and progressive legislation will take place. Among the changes that humans must experience is that such participation is a fundamental necessity like food and water for stable and secure lives. True democracy then takes on the character of a needed result.

Just as exercise and a proper diet promote good health, participation promotes good government. And we need government to function in a way that allows it to be formed and controlled democratically. For example, national involvement should not attempt to handle every issue that arises in every place. The principle of subsidiarity reflects that limit on national government. True democracy also limits it because a large nation of hundreds of millions of citizens cannot and will not spend the enormous amount of time and effort it would take to make such decisions.

Conservatives are right in wanting to limit what a national government can do because elected officials and their appointed agents have the same limits of knowledge about every location and its needs. But people living reasonably near one another do know the conditions and needs they share even when their conditions and needs differ from those of people living elsewhere in the same country.

True democracy works best locally, so localism makes up one of its ingredients. What we share locally far exceeds what we share nationally despite the overselling of nationalism as patriotism and the focus of news on persons in national governmental offices. News reporters and particularly those on television believe that reporting from the White House makes them appear more important than those reporting from city hall. Since that appearance of importance attaches to the news agency, the television network, or to the newspaper covering such news, they practice it daily, drawing attention to the dramatic nature of their subject without the details that would inform readers and viewers. At the same time, they are neglecting coverage that informs the public of the local situation on which they could act together.

News coverage shapes the story Korten refers to in *The Great Turning*. We would do well to learn more about good journalism and choose news sources that practice it rather than the trite rule "If it bleeds, it leads." That it relates to television news, a practice that has continued for a long time, should tell us that TV is not a good source for news and that we should watch it less if at all. While printed news has adopted the principle to some extent because of its competition with television, large losses of television news audiences should lead newspaper policies to reduce or abandon the practice of exciting nonjournalism.

Has the rise of social media changed this? Perhaps serious blogs that go more deeply into their subjects can make a difference. But the popular media, Facebook, Twitter, and the like appear not to improve the situation but to make it worse. I think that is because popular media allow individuals to compete for attention and so many do so by coming up with flashy ways of expressing themselves on topics that need careful research and development. And some of them share the motivation that leads to excessive White House coverage—To be near the president is to be important. That might explain why the most followed Twitter account in 2020 was that of former president Barack Obama, who had nearly 130 million followers. Other celebrities have high followings also on Facebook and Instagram like Christiano Ronaldo, a Portuguese footballer. Evidently, this area has some of the same influences as television such as the human curiosity about exciting or frightening stories about important people arising out of human weakness and fear.

In previous decades, the journalistic mission was to report the news as it actually happened with fairness, balance, and integrity. However, capitalistic motives associated with journalism have forced much of today's television news to look to the spectacular, the stirring, and the controversial as news stories. It's no longer a race to break the story first or get the facts right. Instead, it's to acquire good ratings in order to get advertisers so that profits soar. *Psychology Today* has a story explaining why this is the case.[56]

> The extent media has gone to includes hiring consultants who offer fear-based topics that are pre-scripted, outlined with point-of-view shots, and have experts at-the-ready ... This practice is known as stunting or just-add-water reporting. Often, these practices present misleading information and promote anxiety in the viewer.[57]

---

[56] *If It Bleeds, It Leads: Understanding Fear-Based Media.* By Deboah Serani, PsyD. Available at www.psychologytoday.com/us/blog/two-takes-depression/201106/if-it-bleeds-it-leads-understanding-fear-based-media.

[57] Ibid.

I have often thought that the news being presented placed more emphasis and dedicated more time to apparently rehearsed dialogues between reporters and mainly professors or former officials. The answers given appear not to be off the cuff but prepared and delivered separately from when asked. They often respond to the question, "How did you feel when you learned that ...?" Often, the answer is too well organized to have been a spontaneous reaction to the question. Generalizations and lack of facts characterize so much of the news that it fails to inform. And the same story is often repeated day after day with slight modifications to make it appear to be news but not meeting the standard of what we once experienced as news.

Far too much of it concerns what has come to be called the horse race, political opposition and the effects of statements and decisions on the chances of a politician being elected or reelected. After a presidential election and the winner's taking office, the topic used to be dropped from the news. We would not hear about the next election, four years off, until about three years later. Now, the topic is taken up even before the president-elect is sworn in. What the president and other elected officials will say and do now depends more on their effects on a party's chances of winning future elections and the speaker's/actor's chances of winning again rather than on the consequences of policy on the lives of the governed. Partisanship stands out as the primary concern of the speaker with the terms *Democrats* and *Republicans* often bandied back and forth to the point that you realize that it is the real subject, not public policy. They represent their party as intelligent, capable, ethical, and concerned about people while representing the opposition as stupid, self-serving, and a threat to the country.

The most common reason given for backing or opposing some proposal concerns its supposed effect on job creation. The most wealth-concentrating proposals will supposedly create jobs. They ignore the reality that people, even poor people, can create their own jobs by undertaking action with others to create small businesses that will support them. That such jobs don't promise a future of high wealth for those creating them doesn't matter. The jobs created and owned by big business don't even assure their recipients of avoiding a life of poverty and overwork. That even those jobs would be created is merely a claim backed by no evidence. Given that increasing employment reduces unemployment and places pressure on employers to raise wages, the claim of creating more jobs runs counter to the proven interests of big business—to keep unemployment high so that they can keep wages low and profits high. That is an unfair form of competition in which the true owners of jobs compete not just with other employers but also with workers for ownership of the value created by work. We do not hear of corporations competing with their employees, but we should. It is an example of what President Biden meant when he said, "Capitalism without competition isn't capitalism. It's exploitation." He meant that the excessive competition of some eliminates competitors and produces the concentration of wealth we have now. It allows large capitalist firms to exploit their customers and employees.

Worker-owned businesses also compete but not against each other and their owners. They limit their competition by emphasizing cooperation and by remaining aware of the local community and its needs. They do not try to become monopolists as many capitalists do.

As worker cooperatives grow in number and become recognized as an important and highly beneficial form of business, they will help change the story and the reality about American life. The American dream may begin to incorporate the Mondragon dream, the awareness that in cooperation, workers can have a better life, and drop from the American dream the idea that everyone can become super-rich and that the effort to do so is an example of how we enjoy freedom. This shows the truth of a statement that freedom, although important, has limits that must be observed and acted on.[58]

Ralph Nader has important thoughts about organizing as a democracy. He believes that we need many leaders and that people can join a movement for progress not just as followers but as more leaders of it. Its growth depends on them and the actions they take.[59]

Nader recommends the Citizens Summons as a strategy for constituents to exercise their power and compete with that of the 1 percent who now monopolize the attention of elected representatives. By Citizen Summons he means that a group of citizens plan an event and invite their elected official to attend and to be prepared to answer their questions. His concern for the privatization of airwaves, public land, and mined natural resources agrees with the teaching in *Equal Justice for All* that the earth and its natural resources belong to all of us. He calls the takeover corporatization, not privatization, the term preferred by its beneficiaries. He also uses the term *commons* in the sense of those resources and organizations that should remain in public

[58] John Paul II's encyclical *Veritatis splendor*, section 86.

[59] Ralph Nader's reference to Bill McKibben in *Breaking Through Power*, 94.

ownership. He mentions harms of corporatization as including the earthquakes from fracking in Oklahoma told to me by a sister who suffered from them.

As long as economic prosperity for all continues to be misrepresented as requiring top-down control of business and government and control of government by the 1 percent, we will continue to have large numbers of people in poverty. Nader sees the decline of journalism as one cause of the decline of democracy. Since democracy depends on an informed public, he explores the way combining media and especially television and newspapers has shifted even public television from its ad-free beginnings to domination by its major donors so that there is less reporting of facts and more entertainment, trivia, and focus on dramatic or frightening events. Acceptance of such content derives, he believes, from the passiveness produced in society by its lack of influence over more important social matters.

Another critic of corporate-controlled news media is Gar Alperovitz, a historian and political economist who has written extensively about the need for systemic change to the US system.[60] His major criticism concerns economic domination leading to political domination and the persistence of widespread poverty from it.

In the afterword of *What Then Must We Do?* Alperovitz brings up the need for regional government in a way that appears to support subsidiarity. In *America Beyond Capitalism*, he goes well beyond the theme of my work by dealing with the causes

[60] garalperovitz.org/page/41/?version=meter%20at%20null&module=meter-Links&pgtype=article&contentId&mediaId&referrer&priority=true&action=click&contentCollection=meter-links-click.

of the decline of equality, liberty, and democracy. He mentions subsidiarity as part of the discussion of the need to move some political power to regions of the US because of the inability of local and federal governments to handle some needs. He says,

> The principle of subsidiarity—keeping decision-making at the lowest feasible level, and only elevating it to higher levels when absolutely necessary—is a guiding principle of the model [of decentralization] throughout, a particularly robust discussion of such issues was begun in the 1930s, only to be sidelined by WWII.[61]

This is a rare mention of the term to be encountered in secular writing about the economic, social, and political problems of the US. Alperovitz gives no references to those discussions, but they have been neglected along with the topic of interest.

An important point about subsidiarity is that practiced well and continuously, it would reduce the size of federal government, its budget, and its number of employees and contractors. This ought to satisfy the conservatives who complain of big government. Although it would shift control of local matters to thousands of local governments, they would not need to grow. Their budgets would increase to deal with the current need for improving our neglected and degraded infrastructure.

He mentions the influence of worker-owned businesses on democracy.

---

[61] Gar Alperovitz, *America Beyond Capitalism*, Boston, Democracy Collaborative Press, 2001, xxxiii.

> An important feature of worker-owned firms is that they not only change the ownership of wealth but also are far more anchored in local communities by virtue of the simple fact that worker-owners live in the community.[62]

Its chapter 4 has other references pertinent to worker ownership and democracy.

Chapter 5 tells of the history of regionalism and has numerous references to works telling of our need for it. While it does not present the topic as a matter of morality as is done with subsidiarity, its practical basis shows the consequences of huge government that support the moral argument.

The remainder of the book examines the possibility of democracy becoming more local, of greater government ownership of utilities, and the region becoming an effective level of government. A related topic he presents is the possibility of further gender equality and reduction of racism, and he offers many reasons to support it, but his main point remains the development of equality in the sharing of wealth and political power based on shifting attitudes and recognition of the ability of people to develop and learn along with improvements in education and media use.

A work by Michael J. Sandel contains some discussion of the levels of government relevant to subsidiarity without using the term.[63] Further interest appears in Sandel's discussion of Louis

---

62 Ibid., 49.

63 *Public Philosophy: Essays on Morality in Politics*, Cambridge, Harvard University Press, 2005 See especially pages 29–34.

D. Brandeis and the effect of his political and legal philosophy on American thought. Law students often find Brandeis's Supreme Court opinions more interesting than those of any others on the court.[64] Further research of Brandeis could prove to be of great help in advancing movement to improved government.

In discussing the changes to American political thinking during the Reagan candidacy,[65] Sandel describes his New Federalism in a way that sounds almost like subsidiarity: "a common life of larger meanings on a smaller, less impersonal scale than that the procedural republic provides." New Federalism would "shift power to states and localities" away from "big government" but without reducing the power of big business. This sounds like a step toward subsidiarity, but it does not go far enough by applying it only to government. At the same time, he supported big business with its antisubsidiarity concentration of power producing governmental concentration of power on the federal level.

He refers to the polyarchy of Robert A. Dahl involving the multiplicity of political and moral views that can function in a true democratic republic. In *A Preface to Economic Democracy*, Dahl struggles with the early arguments among writers including Tocqueville and others over the apparent threat of democracy to liberty and property. He recommends worker ownership in its form of worker cooperatives over employee stock ownership plans,

---

[64] Ibid. See pages 14–15 for Sandel's discussion of some of Brandeis's most important thinking on the topic.

[65] Ibid., 22.

which do not create employee control of the corporation.[66] He sees worker cooperatives as another form of democratic organization and mainly considers Mondragon as an example of economic stability.[67]

The discussion of the right to property should be compared with and contrasted to that in *Economic Justice for All.* Locke and Mill have different arguments both of which Dahl rejects. He concludes that none of the arguments justify ownership of corporate enterprise.

> Consequently, the demos and its representatives are entitled to decide by means of the democratic process how economic enterprises should be owned and controlled in order to achieve, so far as may be possible, such values as democracy, fairness, efficiency, the cultivation of desirable human qualities, and an entitlement to such minimal personal resources as may be necessary to a good life.[68]

Contrast this with *Economic Justice for All*, which bases the right to property on moral grounds with a religious origin.

Regarding worker cooperatives, which he calls "self-governing enterprises,"[69] he uses the term *guardianship* in a way that suggests

---

[66] Robert A. Dahl, *A Preface to Economic Democracy*, Oakland, University of California Press,1986, 93.

[67] Ibid., 123.

[68] Ibid., 83.

[69] Ibid., 91.

that it means the opposition to subsidiarity.[70] See the references to subsidiarity in *Economic Justice for All* made by other authors who expand on it and note how it states a connection between subsidiarity and pluralism.

A puzzle: If the shared property of a worker cooperative is not the personal property of worker-owners because no worker-owner has the right to sell his or her share, how does the right to property ownership apply to co-ops? Is there some other way individual worker-owners can be said to own property in the co-op? Or must we just say that it is an instance in which a human who has right of property ownership has elected not to exercise it while retaining it in home ownership, outside savings and investments, and other forms of property? Perhaps we should say that like the property of married couples under California law, ownership need not be only individual; it may be a shared right so that such ownership is joint.

Regarding the puzzle of property in a worker cooperative, the fact that some ownership is shared leaves the possibility that other ownership is not. So member-owners likely have property in their home, savings, and other personal property they would not have as wage slaves.

The principles of worker cooperatives tell us that the right to personal property is not the only property right we have. We also have the right to shared property as described above. Exercised on a small scale as is the case in a cooperative, the right, protected by democratic decision-making, adds to each member's right to personal property.

"The Principle of Subsidiarity as a Constitutional Principle in the

---

[70] Ibid., 94ff.

EU and Canada"[71] contrasts the two interpretations of subsidiarity and shows some of the limitations of invoking the principle.

Also see *Quadragesimo anno* and its limited discussion of property rights as morally based. See no. 138, where the relations between justice, charity, and cooperation remind us of the Family Independence Initiative work to help the poor help themselves to end their poverty. That area of the encyclical mentions cooperation several times.

In speaking of needed economic development of poor countries, Pope John Paul II said,

> Development demands above all a spirit of initiative on the part of the countries which need it. Each of them must act in accordance with its own responsibilities, not expecting everything from the more favored countries, and acting in collaboration with others in the same situation.[72]

This parallels the way the Family Independence Initiative approaches reducing and eliminating family poverty, applying it to the international scene. The encyclical adds,

> The developing nations themselves have the duty to practice solidarity among themselves and with the neediest countries of the world.[73]

---

[71] See article by Andreas Follesdal and Victor Muniz-Fraticelli at researchgate.net/publication/297608715_The_Principle_of_Subsidiarity_as_a_Constitutional_Principle_in_the_EU_and_Canada.

[72] *Sollicitudo rei socialis* (1987), section 44.

[73] Ibid., section 45.

That would not eliminate the responsibility of wealthy nations to engage with them justly, but it tells us that solidarity has dimensions that favor improvement on several levels of organization.

The many sources describing the benefits of challenging the status quo and the neglect of solutions to the problems it has created for many people in the US should alert us to the truth of Nader's assertion that action undertaken to solve the problems will work when people organize to do so.

In the next chapter, we will see how another current movement picks up the themes of this one and advances the steps to improvement.

CHAPTER 5

Localism: The Current Challenge

Localism may be the most complex theme in this book because the term, like the word *democracy*, has so many different meanings. Among them, political philosophy is the most developed meaning, but others such as populism or support "for local food markets, farmers' markets, community-supported agriculture, community gardens, farm-to-table programs, food cooperatives, and restaurants that serve local food"[74] are just some of the preferences of people meant by those who use the term. It also involves "Support for locally owned, independent businesses, including community banks and credit unions …"[75] It can mean localism in media and in government structure, allowing for some independence of small community councils and workers' councils and even religious organizations.[76]

Given the high degree of ambiguity of the term, this document will stress the meanings of localism that reflect the political structure in which the power of local people to deal with local conditions takes preference over attempts to create national standards that do not reflect the differing conditions of localities. Leaving aside religious localism, it will discuss local power, expressed through democracy, to serve the local needs for

---

74 en.wikipedia.org/wiki/Localism_(politics).

75 Ibid.

76 Ibid.

political, economic, and social organization not uniformly spread across a state or nation. In this usage, it forms the pragmatic realization of subsidiarity, the ethical standard it can meet.

The many meanings of the term *localism* derive from the many aspects of local life affecting people and different local conditions that people need to deal with, some more variable than others. Politically, localism refers to the support for local life through more local control and less control by a higher, more extensive authority. Like subsidiarity, it seeks to place some types of power where they can benefit people more. Because localism deals with different topics, for the purposes of this writing, I will deal with that aspect even though it affects and may originate in others such as the preference for locally grown food or local social forms.

David Brooks, in his *New York Times* article "The Localist Revolution" of July 19, 2018, sees localism as a slowly growing revolution that is moving the power away from the centers in nations to the many local places where people live and see the conditions of life in their own families and in those who live near them.

He refers to Deborah Frieze and her TEDx talk in which she adds to the list of new developments such as community land trusts, community-supported agriculture, worker cooperatives, and residential choices that encourage participation and shift power from the overly centralized and corporate-run centers.[77] She describes four roles we can play to deal with a failing major system and replace it with one serving local needs. She describes them as trailblazers, hospice workers, illuminators, and protectors.

One I have tried regarding worker cooperatives involves the

[77] Watch her speech on www.youtube.com/watch?v=2jTdZSPBRRE.

role of illuminators. I have attempted to gain attention for and local knowledge of this mostly unknown business form in the community of Paso Robles, California. What I have learned from my failure to gain the cooperation of the city council tells me that I cannot do it alone but must first associate with others in a joint effort. That effort must be ongoing, not a single project such as my attempt to get the city council to adopt a resolution reflecting the city's support for worker cooperatives. My belief that such a resolution would help spread local knowledge of the form I still take to be true, but I see that it is only one of many possible ways of informing the public, ways I should put into practice. It must include other actions I take with members of a local group aimed at increasing public awareness of the existence and benefits of worker cooperatives.

His article mentions another growing trend, populism. Use of the term *populism* grew out of the farmers' grange movement but has multiple meanings today. Imagine a combination of localism and populism. The former may increase the latter in its original sense. So ambiguous is the term that it has been applied to political candidates of widely different and opposed positions such as Donald Trump and Bernie Sanders.

Another term, *popularism*, further confuses the topic of political positions. Defined as "any political doctrine chosen to appeal to a majority of the electorate," it has more to do with strategy of political campaigns than with the political position described by populism.[78] Distinguishing it from populism can help. A *New York Times* article by Ezra Klein on popularism brings up another

[78] Several internet sources distinguish the two. A good one can be found at maindifference.net/popularism-vs-populism/.

aspect for considering how the public is educated on political matters. In "David Shor Is Telling Democrats What They Don't Want to Hear," Klein (October 8, 2021) prefers to see the problem of Democrats not as popularism but as a term he introduces—*partyism*.[79] Partyism acts as prejudice against persons of a political party different from a majority considering qualifications for jobs, beliefs, or opinions on social and economic matters and others. Like capitalism, it works from the top down, in this case, the political education of most Democrats being controlled by the few. It influences decisions on matters not genuinely political such as employment and membership in organizations, and it acts as prejudice against members of one's opposition party. The positions on issues of those in power differ from those of the majority. Klein sees party politics as national, not local, despite the popular expression "All politics is local." That is another area where subsidiarity should apply.

Tip O'Neill, popularizer of the expression, ran against Frank McNamara in 1982, the Republican candidate for a Massachusetts House of Representatives seat whose campaign was funded most by oil interests in Oklahoma and Texas. That episode in American politics raises again the problem of a false democracy when it depends too much on the gaining of office by large amounts of money and especially of money from nonconstituents. The Russians must have learned from that episode and many others like it. As mentioned before, I was shocked to learn that Susana

---

[79] Klein believes that US politics is excessively national and that it prevents Democrats from taking the positions their members want. The topics its leaders are willing to support are not the topics local people find compelling.

Martinez became governor with the support of oil interests in other states and through a large donation from the Republican Governors Association.

How Can We Promote Genuine Representation of Citizens?

This brings up the topic of clean elections, a highly varied approach to assuring representation of constituents. One article mentions twenty-seven states, counties, and cities with one form or another of promoting funding of elections by constituents.[80] Also called public funding, legislation enacting clean money gives financial support from the state government to candidates who obtain their donations from constituents and turn down donations from nonconstituents. The terms vary in the twenty-seven political authorities that have adopted clean-money legislation, but they appear to be effective.[81] One example, Connecticut, has shown several improvements of democracy because of public funding.[82]

In the more representative national offices, the Senate and especially the House of Representatives, the issue of clean money needs to be applied effectively in all fifty states. The case of *McCutcheon v. the Federal Election Commission* has weakened

---

[80] For data on clean funding of campaigns, see www.demos.org/research/public-funding-electoral-campaigns-how-27-states-counties-and-municipalities-empower-small.

[81] One description of how clean funding works is at www.azcleanelections.gov/run-for-office/how-clean-funding-works.

[82] See www.demos.org/research/fresh-start-impact-public-campaign-financing-connecticut.

democracy by allowing more financial support of candidates from nonconstituent donors.[83] Like subsidiarity, the issue of constituency and campaign financing involves the question of how truly democratic our nation is. In the *Citizens United* case, the Supreme Court pointed to free speech, a constitutional right, as the basis for approval of unlimited spending without constituency and even for corporations. The decision has prevented state action to ensure its local constituency representation and has added to the domination of the country by the wealthy and corporations. It has rendered political localism politically unenforceable except through measures such as clean elections by way of public funding. It has increased the belief that democracy is a national trait without greater intensity on the local level.

As a way of practicing subsidiarity, clean-money campaign funding makes candidates who gain office more dependent on their constituents and frees them from the domination of outsiders, particularly those who represent corporations and their higher-level groups such as an oil producers' association. It would affect other aspects of political, economic, and social life in the country if it became the primary means of financing campaigns. It would reduce the feeling of many citizens that because they have only one vote among many, it is not in their interest to bother to vote. Knowing that by making a small contribution to a candidate along with their neighbors, they could create a way for their candidate to blow the whistle on any opponent who accepts outside funds. Such a candidate could point out the opponent's failure to follow the principle of democratic representation. If I vote for a candidate

---

[83] See "Of Constituents and Contributors" by Richard Briffault of Columbia Law School, brfflt@law.columbia.edu.

whose donors cannot vote for her, I am simply giving away my vote to serve the wishes of someone who is likely to have a grip on the representative of my district as well as on others. Big money hires political servants with their donations, gaining support for their selfish desires by choking off genuine democracy. Outside funding of political campaigns cripples democracy and at the same time corrupts the republican, representative character of our government. Officials elected with outside money come to serve donors, not their constituents.

By dominating large numbers of elected officials, big-money donors make sure that the laws also dominate localities, reduce worker rights and income, and draw money from localities to their deep pockets. They block the will of the people to see such problems as ecological damage from industrial practices solved. They keep the poor in poverty, prevent workers from forming unions, and cause local infrastructure to decay, not only highways and water supply but also education, law enforcement, and health care.

The expression of localism based on subsidiarity improves lives for the many because it allows them to have some control of the local conditions affecting them. At the same time, it allows for the exercise of authority on the state and national levels when and where needed. If it ever becomes the way political life is organized around the world, it will produce peace, reduce military spending, and redirect the wealth produced by workers to local needs.

An academic criticism of subsidiarity, "The Localist Tradition in America," a 2015 PhD dissertation by Trevor Latimer, maintains that it "does not provide its own normative justification."[84] It is true that the encyclical he cites, *Quadragesimo anno*, does not develop its statement defining subsidiarity. But a statement in section 79 compares the immorality of removing autonomy from associations to that of removing it from individuals; it implies a moral basis for subsidiarity in organizations. Without the freedom to act on their own to achieve positive goals, the human right to make decisions would be violated. Applying that situation to the broader context of organizational association makes good sense. It preserves the democracy of subsidiary groups and maintains the right shared by individuals in the groups to make moral decisions.

Latimer later had more to say about subsidiarity. He mentions a later article of his, "The Principle of Subsidiarity: A Democratic Reinterpretation," saying, "I show how subsidiarity can be reinterpreted so as to earn our support."[85] His criticism of the principle in his dissertation does not deal with it as the ethical principle it is but as a structural principle. He denies that it has its own normative justification. I believe the justification is developed beyond the encyclicals he mentions. See *Economic Justice for All*, which presents further justification. Unlike the dissertation, which looks at the principle through the example of the Treaty of Maastricht and the European Union, the latter document concerns itself with human beings and their rights and duties, not just their institutions. And the European Union does not apply a full example of subsidiarity because it concerns there

---

[84] The Latimer dissertation is at dataspace.princeton.edu/bitstream/88435/dsp01794080550/1/Latimer_princeton_0181D_11505.pdf, accessed 1-19-2019.

[85] Latimer's statement in politics.princeton.edu/people/trevor-latimer.

just the relations between it and its member nations. *Economic Justice for All* applies it to all levels of organization and shows how failure to observe it affects people. Applying it can be a challenge, but that does not mean that we are lacking general reasons for assigning authority to lower-level units.

The general reasons have to do with economic justice, a matter that applies to persons, especially in the home and even more significantly to those who are poor or both poor and homeless. How localism helps meet the general reason shows that there are multiple means, one of which is the powerful means of worker cooperatives. As a form of localism guided by subsidiarity, it places the power of decision-making with individuals who work with solidarity for the benefit of all the workers of a firm. By doing so, it supports localism in a most powerful way.

The example of Mondragon and its structure shows how subsidiarity can be applied. Its higher level, Mondragon Corporation, leaves in place the authority of the firms that formed it and has authority to act only as given by its constituent firms. Like them, it is a cooperative and applies democracy in a way that provides the highest benefit to its members and the community where they create wealth.

Among the benefits of a higher number of worker cooperatives in a community as shown in Mondragon is the lack of homelessness and long-term poverty. It also has the lowest crime rate in all Europe. By allowing individuals to cooperate for their personal and joint welfare, it has created a community that serves as an example for other locations to work for beneficial development. But it cannot be done from the top down. Individual workers must come to realize that they have the power to improve their lives by jointly working for their individual and collective welfare. They may not know of subsidiarity by its name, but they apply it in their work.

There are other ways to apply subsidiarity that politicians and others need to be aware of. We need more people to become entrepreneurs, but not the capitalistic types who take advantage of workers, treat them like assets, and draw as much work from them as possible at wages as low as possible to gain as much profit for themselves as possible. A step toward the attempt to justify such poor treatment showed itself when major corporations changed the name of their personnel departments to human resources departments. To name employees in such a way shows that they are considered a means of production and profit just as capital assets are. Immanuel Kant made clear how treating humans merely as means violates morality in which all humans should be treated as ends,[86] as if they and their well-being are the goal of management and its exercise of authority.

In keeping with the Kantian explanation of this aspect of human relations and its basis in justice, worker cooperatives value democracy and equality as conventional businesses do not. We need a greater awareness of the economic justice of the worker-cooperative form of business and a much larger number of such firms. In them, the workers become entrepreneurs, but they are not motivated by greed or the desire for power over others. Such entrepreneurs desire a decent living for themselves, for their joint worker-owners, and for society in general. Their contribution to achieving that desire is well documented in those communities

---

[86] Immanuel Kant, *Groundwork of the Metaphysics of Morals*, Cambridge, Cambridge University Press, 1785, 4:429.

where many businesses are such cooperatives. They contribute to the local communities in which they operate, thus strengthening the acceptance of localism there. They reduce the incidence of violations of subsidiarity because no large entity of concentrated wealth owns them and they supply many of the needs of their community, reducing the opportunity of the big corporations and wealthy individuals to dominate the local economy and its workers.

Respect for worker cooperatives and other forms of cooperative businesses have a close tie to localism as they support and spread it while allowing for any needed contribution to larger forms of economic, social, and political organization. A good example exists in the Emilia-Romagna region of Italy, where small worker cooperatives have learned to join with others to take on projects requiring a wide variety of capabilities that none of them individually possesses. The Bologna-centered collection of such businesses has formed a network of industrial and social cooperatives that produce 30 percent of the region's GDP. The region was affected less by the European debt crisis than was southern Italy, an area with fewer cooperatives. That is true also of Mondragon despite its different organization of cooperatives and appearing to many Americans to be a single entity, the Mondragon Corporation.

An advantage enjoyed by Italians consists of legal support for worker cooperatives; several laws help advance the creation and maintenance of such businesses.[87] To its credit, the US and California now have laws that do that to some extent, making co-op creation more advantageous than before. Yet the US has only about 7,000 members of its less than 400 worker cooperatives. Compare that to Italy with its 25,000 worker cooperatives providing decent livings to its members.

What does this have to do with localism? Since localism is not simply about politics, it has a great deal to do with how businesses are structured and operated. Would it be possible to operate a national or international capitalist business corporation in a way that respects and implements localism? Hardly. The very existence and goals of the highest level of management prevent that from happening. The main goal there is the achievement of profit in the short term for the benefit of capital investors and for the managers whose high salaries and bonuses are tied to profit.

When return on investment is more important than the welfare of employees and the communities where they live, the application of subsidiarity plays no role in decisions made on the highest level. Those decisions get carried down through the hierarchy of management to the lowest level of management, where they are imposed on nonmanagement employees. It has given rise to the term *wage slaves* for their role. They are said to be fortunate to have jobs, but as mentioned before, they do not have jobs. If they did have them, if their jobs were their property,

---

[87] One of its laws, the Marcora Law, allows workers who lose their jobs in capitalist firms to receive their future unemployment insurance payments in a single payment if they will form a worker cooperative with others so situated. Their combined receipts help avoid the problem of initial funds for the new business.

they would not do away with them to increase stock value. Nor would they move them to another location, to another country even based on lower taxes there or lower incomes.

It is more accurate to say that the corporations have the jobs. They create them, destroy them, move them, and reward them as their managers see the need to promote the goal of investor profit. When Walmart closes a store in a small town, its former employees might move to another location, but who pays the cost of their moving? Some will simply be out of work. Walmart does not consider employees who become jobless and face a situation in which a replacement job is not at hand. Nor does Walmart worry about the effect of the loss of employment income on the community where the store had been. The suddenly impoverished former employees will not be able to support other businesses and social institutions to which they had formerly contributed. Their lower tax payments will reduce the state and local basis for supporting infrastructure, allowing it to deteriorate and thus harm other members of the community.

Locally owned businesses and especially those created by residents as individuals or partnerships have an option for dealing with their need to retire. They can simply sell the business to their employees as part of its becoming a worker cooperative. A movement is underway in the US to assist in the process needed to make the conversion from being privately owned to being cooperatively owned. Organizations in the movement teach students and inform the public about the advantages of employee ownership. [88] They maintain websites to spread the word, they hold workshops, and they provide information to business owners on business-ownership options. The support by government and NGOs in this area of enterprise helps increase localism. Done frequently enough, it can change communities to the extent achieved in Mondragon and Emilia-Romagna. This will not occur overnight; it may take many decades just as the growth of cooperatives in those two examples took place slowly.

The support of localism in the US has grown in the areas of locally grown foods, support for locally owned businesses, and participation in local events. It still has far to grow before its effects on national politics will be visible. As we learn more about its many ramifications, our commitment to it will increase. The word will spread as Deborah Frieze has pointed out. And as it does, support will grow, and supporters will organize to work together to make its benefits a growing trend.

I heard a speech given by Dr. Martin Luther King Jr. entitled "What Is Your Life's Blueprint?" in which he encouraged young

---

[88] National organizations and regional/local organizations working to help create worker-owned businesses as ESOPs and worker cooperatives. Among the national organizations are the National Center for Employee Ownership (NCEO), the Beyster Institute at the University of California at San Diego, the Democracy Collaborative, and the Curriculum Library for Employee Ownership at Rutgers University. Some of the local ones are the New Jersey/New York Center for Employee Ownership, the Indiana Center for Employee Ownership, the Vermont Employee Ownership Center, the Pennsylvania Center for Employee Ownership, and the Ohio Employee Ownership Center at Kent State University.

people to consider the values they were adopting.[89] Although the speech did not mention cooperation, others did. Most likely, he would have been a supporter of worker cooperatives. He saw the need for individuals to join together and act as a group for the benefit of all its members. He referred to sit-ins as an example of persistent activity toward a goal that had been successful. It brought about a major change in the social laws regarding integration although the movement at the time of the speech had regrettably declined in its effectiveness and white supporters of Selma, Alabama, were not standing up to protect African Americans and other minorities.

He referred to democracy in the Selma speech. Because worker cooperatives have democracy as a major principle, surely he would have supported the form, if not in that speech, in others if he was aware of them. At that time, they were not a well-known form of business in this country. And there is still a low level of awareness of their existence and benefits. We still have a lot to do to encourage workers to increase the number of them and knowledge of them among the public. That effort as well is being undertaken by organizations such as the US Federation of Worker Cooperatives and such organizations in regions such as California Center for Cooperative Development and the Valley Alliance of Worker Cooperatives in the New England area. Such organizations help spread the word and help groups form new cooperatives.

Another contributor to the localism movement is a form of residence called cohousing, mentioned above. It is relatively new

[89] Available at www.youtube.com/watch?v=ZmtOGXreTOU. He spoke at Barratt Junior High School in Philadelphia on October 26, 1967.

in this country and is still developing its features to meet its goal of neighbors being more aware of one another and interacting with one another in ways that benefit them all. While many cohousing communities have conflicts over policy among their members, their effort to work together to resolve them shows that they understand that it is up to them to settle the conflicts and organize in a way that will prevent differences from arising as often as they do now.

The work of Mauricio Miller in *The Alternative: Most of What You Believe about Poverty Is Wrong* also contributes to localism. His insistence that an organization attempting to help the poor by getting them to lift themselves out of poverty by working cooperatively with other poor families in their area shows his understanding that equality of wealth depends on local efforts and not some national law. The work done by the Family Independence Initiative and its successor, UpTogether, has proven effective for many people. Gang membership among the young has been reduced in areas such as the poorest part of Oakland, California, by giving the young a different path to follow and a greater sense of personal worth.

One effect noted by Miller in his book tells how the Iu Mien community organized itself to deal with the problem of their children joining gangs and breaking the law. They worked together to get their children to attend college and to improve their economic lives. The approach proved to be a great benefit to the younger generations and brought the parents involved in organizing it to a greater sense of their own values in organizing and cooperating with one another.[90]

Localism is connected to patriotism when that word is properly understood. The widespread practice of calling nationalism patriotism has led most Americans away from true patriotism to the support of a militaristic and imperial nation dominated by wealthy corporations heading us down the road to destruction of the environment and the perpetuation of poverty and crime. By calling American militarism patriotism, it attempts to justify the intervention of the country in the local matters of foreign countries. It seeks to make the invention and development of new deadly weapons a sign of patriotism even though the true motive for that activity is the concentration of wealth in so-called defense spending. By calling the wearing of a military uniform a sign of patriotism, it encourages the young to give up on more education and place themselves in military institutions, where they learn the harsh techniques their commanders use to enforce their obedience or to subjugate others as ranking above them. It has become the most constantly taught lesson of basic military training. Trainees learn to snap to attention and to obey any command given without taking time to think about it and its ethical basis let alone to discuss it with its source.

If defense were truly the goal and not offense against other nations, it could be carried out by local groups working together and serving their families and one another to keep their communities safe. Given sufficient scale of that kind of behavior, peace would replace the belief that our nation needs to

---

[90] Mauricio L. Miller, *The Alternative: Most of What You Believe about Poverty Is Wrong*, Morrisville, North Carolina, Lulu Publishing, 103.

be the most effective killing and destroying organization. A well-developed consideration of these matters tells us that we need to work together locally and more broadly to replace that belief with belief and action to end international threats and war. "Recognize that peace is the wholeness created by right relationships with oneself, other persons, other cultures, other life, Earth, and the larger whole of which all are a part."[91]

[91] Earth Charter, principles III, 16, f.

CHAPTER 6

The Imperfection of True Democracy

The rankings of nations on democracy show none as being perfect. The closest to being perfect, Denmark, ranked by the Democracy Matrix at the University of Würzburg, has a total value index of 0.958, Norway an index of 0.956, and Finland and Sweden at 0.946. All these are in the category of Working Democracy, but no nation has a ranking of 1.00, which would describe a perfect democracy.

This source, ww.democracymatrix.com/ranking, shows the US as a Deficient Democracy with a ranking of 0.811 and having thirty-five nations ranked above it in the Working Democracy category. Rankings by other institutions and on other aspects of comparison give the US different positions compared to the other nations. For example, the Best Countries report ranks Canada number one in Best Overall and does not place the US in the top five. Other rankings place Japan as number one in Entrepreneurship and the US as number one in Power and Agility.

Since we are primarily concerned here with democracy, the points to keep in mind are the lower ranking of the US in democracy and the lack of perfection of even the most highly ranked. Its position as just below the last nation ranked as a Working Democracy suggests that we do not have too far to improve to enter that category. That tells us that there are ways in which democracy can be improved here.

But what accounts for the lack of perfection of all nations? And do we have an idea how one would describe a democratically perfect society? Would it be as large as a nation-state? What would it value, and how would it live by its values? Many questions arise when we attempt to describe such a nation. The closest to perfection has been achieved not in a nation but in some cantons of Switzerland.[92]

Offered as the principles of democracy are freedom, equality, public access, and participation. This is found in an article at the SWI Swissinfo.ch by Claude Longchamp, a political scientist. The article, "The perfect democracy does not exist—not even in Switzerland,"[93] denies that democracy began in Greece and limits it to national governments, making its adoption much later in history. It reviews the changes in the rankings of nations as their forms of democracy changed.

Further research reveals a lot of disagreement over the question of what would constitute perfect democracy. A Wikipedia article points to the variety of meanings of the term *democracy* and the instances where it applies. It sees the Swiss canton as an example of democracy in a nation of cantons and calls it "a semi-direct democracy (representative democracy with strong instruments of direct democracy)."[94]

---

[92] Wikipedia article, en.wikipedia.org/wiki/Switzerland#Politics.

[93] www.swissinfo.ch/eng/directdemocracy/swiss-democracy-in-an-international-context_the-perfect-democracy-does-not-exist---not-even-in-switzerland/45578888.

[94] Wikipedia article, en.wikipedia.org/wiki/Direct democracy.

If the most highly ranked democracy is less than a pure or perfect democracy, what accounts for its slight imperfection? Some is due to the lack of agreement as to what constitutes democracy. Experts on the subject disagree even though they make involvement of the public an essential element. But even the size or configuration of the public can be at issue. For some, it is local, and for others, it can be national. And the principle of participation based on the equality of all citizens lacks an agreed standard. Must 50 percent or more of citizens participate in elections to meet a standard definition? If that were the case, the US could not be called a democracy between 1916 and 2012. In its recent elections, the turnout has been higher and an improvement of American democracy, but it has not earned the nation the highest ranking among nations on other, more general terms. Given the recent increase in gerrymandering and the denial of voting rights to minorities, it would appear that the nation is moving away from democracy toward autocracy. Longchamp accuses the US and other nations of making that move.

If we were able to agree as a nation of citizens and elected officials on the changes needed to move our nation much closer to what would make it a perfect democracy, we know that it would still be somewhat imperfect. First, we would have to agree on the values and principles it would have to display and that we would have to live by. Then we would have to take the steps to make the improvements needed to reach the goal. Doing so would involve a great deal of work on the part of educators, citizens' groups, and business customers to replace the domination by major companies with local businesses in which many would work as owners. It would take a long time to reach agreement on the characteristics of such government and more time to implement the changes needed to make it a reality.

Even then I would not expect democracy to be perfect. Just getting to a level of agreement needed as a major step would not allow us to reach consensus. Having worked in an organization that requires consensus for major changes, I have seen that reaching true consensus of all members is rare. In the organization, such decisions are possible, but I have yet to see a single one in which true consensus showed up. So, it would be good to make decisions by consensus when possible, but to make needed decisions democratically by majority rule when consensus is not a possibility. That would encourage more participation in meetings for decisions and might on occasion lead to some made by consensus.

Imagine for a moment an age in which the vast majority of nations have near-perfect democracies. That they would not be perfect should come as no surprise. Even eliminating militarism, imperialism, and corporate greed, such nations would still have to deal with a simple fact about humanity. We are not perfect. We make mistakes. We are sinners, and some of us are possessed of a degree of selfishness that will not disappear. We lack the knowledge necessary to understand the needs of all people under all circumstances. Many of us do not develop past the imperial consciousness that occurs as a natural development over time. In the understanding of David Korten's book, we see that many remain in that stage far too long and gain power in full adulthood. They do not advance to social consciousness as early as they should so that they become the dominant class of citizens. Their concept of justice is reciprocal— "Do unto me and I will do unto you"—even if the object of reciprocity is hurtful.

If that were to improve and if far fewer adults remained on that level, we would still be a species that makes mistakes and lacks perfect knowledge. So, our democracy would remain imperfect. Human imperfection would continue to infect our social, economic, and political lives.

But even then, we could accept democracy as the best form of government. By reducing the faults now so obvious and so widespread, we would be able to concentrate on other human needs without the neglect of government we now experience. Families would be stronger, better at caring for the young, and contribute more to their communities. Communities would become the centers of many decisions and practices affecting them now being dictated from outside. Solidarity and cooperation would increase as major characteristics of human society on all levels. Instead of the large number of citizens who do not accept governing as it is done, most would accept it because it would promote the benefits of individuals and communities. Those benefits would show in many ways that could be seen and replace the pretenses of benefits repeated as justifications for bad policies and concentrated power. It would be accepted as the best form of government humans are capable of creating despite their individual imperfections. We would be happier to live with it and to deal with it.

It might even lead to a situation where so much improvement in our collective weaknesses has been overcome that we could spend more time and resources getting rid of or reducing our personal faults and weaknesses that hamper us. And even though such an improvement would not necessarily lead to perfection of humans, it would be welcomed as further evidence of the superiority of democracy when it is genuine and supported.

Reaching such a stage would involve a major change in the way of life we now experience. It has been described as a simple way of life in which many provide for their own needs with much less access to the market. People would live in simpler homes with fewer possessions, raise more of their own food, and spend time at tasks that were once left to servants to perform. Some criticize such a way of life as a deterioration from the current way of life. Yet who believes that our current way of life is perfect or beneficial for everyone? I believe that the criticisms of needed improvements based on such a change are wrong. They describe it as involving a return to an earlier, less civilized way of life, an idea that some reject as repeating some bad human history.

Yet the advocates of localism and a truer democracy see such developments as improvements to our way of life without claiming that they could constitute a final or permanent form. To do so would be to imply the end of human creativity. Along with the imperfections that we all carry, some more than others, creativity shows itself in many individuals in many ways. We have no reason to believe that it would be eradicated.

But suppose that instead of adopting a more simple, local, and democratic way of life, some creative genius proposed another new and improved way of life that humans could adopt. Since I cannot describe such a way of life without being that genius, I can only suggest its possibility. But any familiarity with the weaknesses of human nature should warn us that such a development would not change that nature. And while it might be better than any form of government history has given us, we should not believe that it would constitute a perfect democracy.

We cannot act rationally on what we don't know, but what we do know about our situation is that it has the great faults described in the first chapter and that those faults can be reduced if we cooperate to take action to put in place the improvements that help us all and especially those whose lives are made miserable by the concentration of wealth and power and the imposition of government from a distance.

Chapter 4 describes the worker cooperative form of business and its potential widespread adoption as a major improvement needed to move us toward a better way of life generally. But even if that occurred, we would still have an imperfect human nature. That is evident in cooperatives where some cannot always accept the decisions of the majority, some abandon the form, and some even fail. Despite that, their history shows them to be a great improvement over the capitalistic, authoritarian form of big business presently dominating the great majority of peoples' lives. This tells us that even though they would not be perfect, they represent such great improvement that we should work to make them a bigger part of economic life where they are missing. We need them especially in the US, where corporate domination has produced poverty and homelessness for so many that we fail to see them as victims but instead view them as incompetent.

So let us abandon the notion that an improved system must be perfect if it is to be justified. The depth of our problems and the availability of known improvements should move us to action. That recommendation, made by many including Dr. Martin

Luther King Jr., stands as an important principle we should make visible on a wide basis. From his experience in traveling in the US and seeing so much avoidable poverty he said, "I have just been in the process of touring many areas of our country and I must confess that in some situations I have literally found myself crying."[95] He also lamented the poverty he saw in other countries including India, where a large part of the population slept on the streets at night instead of in homes since they had none. We know of such occurrences in this country. And whether knowing of them leads us to crying or not, it should lead us to helpful action. We should not be deterred from acting because the improvements to be made would not make the system perfect. We should deal with imperfection when we see it and not because we fear it.

We can and should accept the way of life that important material, social, and spiritual improvement offers. When we see that our personal benefits may be small but that the benefits to the severely unfortunate may be great, we should work to make the changes that will follow from success of action. We will be accepting a way of life that is less than perfect but much better than what now dominates the country. Doing so would involve the honesty that our current powers lack when they praise the country as an economic wonder while overlooking the problems causing many to suffer and some to die from avoidable causes. When the features of the economy they praise benefit only the few wealthy and result in the poverty of many others, we should expose such features, criticize them, and use the power of democracy to eliminate their dominance. That will produce a nation of greater

[95] The speech can be viewed at seemeonline.com/history/mlk-jr-awake.htm.

wealth for the middle class, fewer poor and homeless, and yes, fewer super wealthy.

It would rely less on national and international stock markets as measures of how well we are doing economically. It would also rely less for that purpose on the GDP. We could produce less overall and yet have more income where it is needed, in the homes of those now suffering from inadequate income. We would produce less waste.[96] We would need to rely less on charitable organizations that currently help bring some to a level of survival without raising them to the level of independence and freedom from future return to the depths of poverty.

The work of Kim Miller should be accepted for inclusion in our general education and understanding of social organization because it works and because it has the needed effect of bringing people together to cooperate for their mutual benefit and for improvement of the communities in which they live. Their discovery of the value of self-help and the way it benefits them when they cooperate to achieve greater equality shows similarity between Up Together and worker cooperatives. Once the poor have learned to rely on one another and on themselves, discovered capabilities they did not know they had, and by putting them to work discover even more, they will find a way of life that allows them to find the values other than economic to enrich their lives. The arts, literature, music, social creativity, and discovery of the values shared in many societies would occupy more of their time as would learning the facts and values of government needed to

[96] "The Story of Stuff," a video by Annie Leonard, describes the causes and consequences of our materialistic society's behavior. It has given rise to a website that expands on the themes she introduced: storyofstuff.org.

motivate participation in democratic action in which voting is an important but only one such activity.

The approach taken by Miller, helping the poor to help themselves, has been recommended in the writings of others. *Economic Justice for All* mentions it in at least three places.[97] Miller might have been aware of it though he does not mention it in his book.

Another benefit of a widespread application of Miller's teaching would be seen in changing a society that has upper and lower classes and where the lower classes are looked down on as a collection of inadequate people, people to be taken advantage of in business, people to be blamed for their inadequacies, and not people with the same dignity as less-afflicted individuals. While there would still be some inequalities of wealth and income, reducing them to the point that they cease to serve the greedy would be acceptable just as an improved but imperfect democracy would be acceptable. Those differences need not be hereditary and most likely would not be.

Notice that even in a worker cooperative, some members earn more than others. They may do so by working longer hours or by having positions of greater education, skill, or responsibility, or by serving as a special part of management. But their greater income is not the basis for domination of other workers. In fact,

[97] "Decisions must be judged in light of what they do for the poor, what they do to help the poor, and what they enable the poor to do for themselves" (section 24). "Therefore, we should seek solutions that enable the poor to help themselves through such means as employment. Paternalistic programs which do too much for and too little with the poor at to be avoided" (section 188). "Grassroots efforts by the poor themselves, helped by community support, are indispensable" (section 357).

cooperatives set limits on how much higher their salaries can be. In Mondragon, it is limited to ten times the average of others. But in our corporate jungle, it runs to hundreds of times the average wage and includes huge bonuses, tax breaks, and government incentives that ordinary workers do not receive.[98]

In employee income, nearly perfect equality results from the democracy of worker cooperatives. It places in the hands of a majority the power to set limits on income inequality and even to remove managers from their positions without necessarily removing them from the firm. Is allowing some income inequality a violation of the values of cooperatives? Since equality is one of them, you might think so. But like the imperfection of the best political democracy, we can accept such imperfection of equality because it does not lead to the harsh and damaging inequality that currently dominates our economic system. Slight imperfection in one aspect of a way of life can lead to great improvement in other, more critical ones.

Notice that accepting the worker cooperative as the best way we know of now for organizing a business does not mean we simply accept its faults when the member-owners fail to live up to the principles of standards of the form. We accept the form because of its superiority over the other forms we have created historically.

Likewise, simply accepting democracy as the best form of government until a better one is discovered does not mean we accept its imperfections. We accept it despite its imperfections,

---

[98] The ratio of CEO compensation to that of typical workers has grown to over 300 in 2020. See the Economic Policy Institute article at epi.org/publication/ceo-pay-in-2020.

knowing that they derive from our imperfections and that we can work together to reduce if not eliminate them. It becomes a journey of each life involving growth in the values we know make for a stronger, more just, and more equitable society. By focusing on a timely advancing in the states of consciousness and helping the young to recognize those stages in themselves and others would reduce the proportion of those caught in the state of imperial consciousness so long that they become a serious problem for themselves and society. Helping them move out of that stage into the state of social consciousness and then into the state of cultural consciousness would increase the influence of the latter two on the social, economic, and political values of a society like ours in the areas where we most need improvement.

Should we attempt to advance individuals through the stages by government action? I doubt it. Some of the most effective effort must come in the home and in early education. Parents who have developed into a social or cultural consciousness would make better teachers of their children and allow them to learn by observing the behavior and heeding what their parents tell them. Government, especially the national government, is too far away to be such a teacher. And in the US, its own problems have some roots in the imperial consciousness that is behind many of its policies. So, it cannot teach by example at the present time. And even when greatly improved, it would still not be the teacher of choice because of its lack of daily contact and exhibited concern for the basic needs of the young, needs best met by their parents and local social organizations: a home, nourishment, affection, care, and concern for growth, safety, and solidarity. To try to make the federal government the solution would violate the principle of subsidiarity and would not succeed.

School teachers should also take some responsibility for advancing the understanding of children of social consciousness and serve as a different example for them. Many do it each day. They make it a part of classroom instruction, and when needed, the private instruction of a misbehaving child. We know that when such instruction is repeated by several persons, two parents and many teachers over the years of greatest development and need, it has great power to help children form the attitudes and understanding they will need as adults. It would help more of them someday reach the fifth state, spiritual consciousness. In that stage, they might become the evolutionary cocreators of an improving society. We have seen such examples as Martin Luther King Jr., David Korten, Kim Miller, and others in earlier years. We need more of them.

We have no clear conception of what would constitute perfect democracy. But knowing the faults of ours, areas needing improvement the most, and ways to achieve that, we have the responsibility to improve it.

CHAPTER 7

The Need for Democracy on All Levels of Government

We have seen how important democracy is for a nation. Its importance became more apparent as the Industrial Revolution took root and moved new nations away from their original state of democracy. This has been most apparent in the US, where concentrations of wealth and power have weakened democracy to the point that those few enjoying their positions have had to hide its lack from those suffering from domination.

Chapter 3 presented other forms of harm now being experienced and their increased seriousness for the US and other nations. Some concerned authors see the uncorrected condition as leading to a catastrophic end of human civilization and possibly human life on earth. Ecological destruction, war, increasing distrust between nations, and the spread of disease, family instability, and education all threaten us.

We need to take seriously the work of David Korten, *The Great Turning*, and Chalmers Johnson, *Nemesis*. These works and others show how we are heading toward annihilation because we allow social, political, and economic characteristics of modern life to take us there. They plead with us to find a better way of life, and they mention some of the features of such a way. They also encourage us to find additional ways to promote the stability and longevity of human life and that of the planet.

Chapter 4 tells of historically recent efforts to deal with the growing problem of the loss of true democracy and presents even a moral standard that would need to be enacted to make acceptable improvement and put a stop to the decline. Chapter 5 discusses localism and the role it should play in an improvement of democracy. We can do so even though an improved democracy would still have imperfection as shown in chapter 6.

Lest we believe that the application of subsidiarity would put an end to national government and change the political structure of a nation to that of completely independent localities, we need to recognize that democracy can and should exist on all levels of government. What are those levels, and how does democracy differ in them?

Democracy in the Home

We can begin with the home. That seems unlikely since the home, while being an economic entity, is not a political entity. So how can democracy apply there?

In many families, it does apply in part as a teaching device and in part as a way of making decisions that reduce conflict. I am referring to those times when a family is about to engage in an activity requiring decisions to be made such as what restaurant to go to for dinner. A family could put that to a vote; parents could solicit their children's suggestions to include them in the decision-making process. It also sets the example for them to follow of considering the desires of others in many situations. They would learn to avoid having to choose either dominating others or being subservient to others. So, families could practice a modest, informal type democracy without parents losing their positions of authority and responsibility for their children.

When children become adults, their relationships with their parents change. They have rights to make decisions and the freedom to enact them. While still members of a family, they must be consulted by their parents about decisions affecting them. Those decisions can be made in a democratic way even if they occur less frequently.

When children reach adulthood and take on the responsibilities and benefits of regular work, the lessons in democracy they learned in their families will help them understand why work should be democratic in some ways home life was not. Having participated in family decision-making, they would know the difference between employment in which they can be treated like pawns and employment in which they can share with other workers management duties and an equitable distribution of pay. The worker cooperative would take on a few of the characteristics of a second home, a place where all care about the others and work for their mutual benefit. It would be a place of continued learning about matters that allow the individual to grow beyond servitude to a greater social awareness and the business skill of entrepreneurship. It would allow them to avoid that condition described by Adam Smith in *An Inquiry into the Nature and Causes of the Wealth of Nations*.

> The man whose whole life is spent in performing a few simple operations, of which the effects are perhaps always the same, or very nearly the same, has no occasion to exert his understanding or to

> exercise his invention in finding out expedients for removing difficulties which never occur. He naturally loses, therefore, the habit of such exertion, and generally becomes as stupid and ignorant as it is possible for a human creature to become. The torpor of his mind renders him not only incapable of relishing or bearing a part in any rational conversation, but of conceiving any generous, noble, or tender sentiment, and consequently of forming any just judgment concerning many even of the ordinary duties of private life.[99]

Adam Smith's words could well have been advocating for worker cooperatives in which the workers develop themselves and the skills suppressed by many of the jobs people take today because they are seen as the only work available for them.

Democracy in the workplace can be considered a continuing gift from each worker-owner to the others and a treasure to the individual. This says nothing about the benefits of such a form of work to the community. That too becomes part of the motivation of the worker missing in contemporary work relations. The growing preference for localism helps workers who encounter their customers' experiences and the benefit of their work. It further strengthens their commitment to the way of life it involves. They develop an appreciation for the greater trust customers have for their organizations and their motivation. By embracing the values and principles of cooperatives, they continue to develop psychologically, advancing in the social and cultural consciousness

---

[99] Book V, chapter 1, 458.

toward the spiritual consciousness, the highest of the five stages of human development.

That experience, part of the continuing education of the worker, helps educate those who encounter such businesses and learn why they are so effective. It can motivate dominated employees to move from their capitalist firms and enter the world of greater cooperation. The flower of cooperatives would bloom in the US as it has in Italy, Mondragon, and elsewhere.

We should consider pertinent differences between the home, business, and political entities. Some of the characteristics of the home are well known to most people, but they need to be presented here so that we better understand how change affects the development of the awareness of and appreciation for democracy.

Over time, the structure of the family changes. Children add to the size and complexity of family relations and duties. As they grow older, they eventually leave home and render it a smaller and operationally different entity. Most of them create new families and with homes, where the teaching of democracy becomes another possibility. And many continue to interact with their parents in ways that require joint decisions. Similarly, a worker cooperative changes over time, giving its members opportunities to change what they produce, how they produce it, and how they relate to other businesses they deal with. While the practices like democracy might remain much the same in the home, true democracy in the cooperative enterprise will strengthen as members learn more about its benefits and ways to implement it. Positions of responsibility may shift as some take on more-detailed exercise of management and some develop new intellectual and craft skills to make their work more productive and valuable to the firm. Through democratic action, the structure of the firm slowly changes.

The natural changes of the family and the democratically selected changes of the worker cooperative differ in that the latter are institutional arrangements based on a matured human nature while the former occur regardless of human choice. A family will eventually disappear with the death of its members. But an institution like a business firm can long outlive its members, allowing the democratic choices to continue and to have a longer-term effect on the business and the community in which it operates.

True political structures last even longer than businesses. When I was a child, S.H. Kress, Montgomery Ward, J.C. Penney, and Sears Roebuck were some of the main stores in our little town and around the country. Where are they now?

For nations, we should consider the possibility that changes to their geographic structure should come more from democratic choice than from the violence of war and the decisions of imperial autocrats. We can see the benefits of a political structure that includes local communities, regions, states, and the nation. For any one combination of these in a particular nation, the exercise of democracy differs in the world. Some nations are more democratic than others because they have kept important local matters on the local level and have given authority to a higher level of organization only when it is necessary and beneficial to lower levels of political entities. They have made a practice of localism, for some motivated by subsidiarity.

Examples of political structures changed through violence and failure are many. The destruction of the Greek and Roman

Empires cost many lives, and the latter cast Western society into the Dark Ages. In modern times, these include the breakdown of the British Empire, the reduced colonization of Africa by European nations,[100] the breakup of Nazi Germany's empire in Europe, and dissolution of the Soviet Union. However, an effort to reverse the loss of geographic locations under the control of Russia is now underway involving Crimea and now Ukraine, creating a dangerous situation that many fear will lead to a broader war, one that could involve the nations in possession of nuclear weapons.

We are missing a procedure that would bring flexibility to the structure of political arrangements of this type and allow change to occur based on the peaceful application of democratic choice. Such a procedure would look at the desires and reasons of people in local areas and take into consideration the benefits of a rearrangement to them and their neighbors. It would examine the benefits of changing the boundaries of political regions based on their relation to local communities and their places in a national structure. The borders of the states here in the US might change; people have recommended that California become two states because of its large population and economic power, which is larger than that of many nations.

It might even involve other nations in the decision-making process if their involvement was peaceful and based on more than their own benefit. While we have no global government per se,

---

[100] The Berlin Conference of 1884–1885 did not end imperialism in Europe even though six of the twenty-seven participating nations ended their colonization in Africa. See en.wikipedia.org/wiki/Berlin_Conference#cite_ref-TC_14-0.

it might even be possible to create one with extremely limited powers and to have it become involved in an advisory way in such matters. Even the United Nations, by its own admission, is not a state or a government.

It is not my intention to redesign the political world. Rather, I offer for consideration the possibility that reshaping it politically through choices made by affected people could replace imperialism and war as the major ways to do that. The actual changes might take a long time to be fashioned and for agreement on a particular change to be accepted by a majority of those affected. The basis for such a change would probably include more than economic effects. It might have to pass tests of sustainability, justice, and equality while rejecting the manipulation of political power achieved through gerrymandering and the grouping of people to isolate some races. It would have to pass the test of truth, especially the truth of avoiding persuasion by the current practice of twisting language to misrepresent reality.

Natural borders would continue to affect the shape of many political units. Rivers (whose change of paths could move the border between adjoining units), mountains, and oceans would be considered. Perhaps the distance of Alaska and Hawaii from the US mainland would come up in such discussions. And even migration could be part of the process of deciding. Since the US is a nation of migrants, those who came from outside its borders and those who migrated westward although born in another state, it should not be overlooked.

The complexity of such decisions would require the development of political science beyond its current stage. It would also involve a major change in education to allow the changes to find a home in the minds of ordinary people and a new body of experts who were deeply embedded in the history of humanity and its organization in politics. It would need to activate a greater awareness of and care for the benefits to society as a whole and reject the concentration of those benefits in particular nations. It would end the contest for gaining our wealth by taking the wealth of other nations or states. And it would have to end the contest for wealth of sustaining its concentration in the hands of the few powerful corporations and their owners.

But change is certain to come. The question we face has to do with the acceptability of such changes and the role more people can play in making them. Would it give rise to a new science? I think so. It would certainly change political science. It would have to change the way such matters are presented by politicians and those with economic and social power. Desirable change would include the development of democracy and the skills it requires among the people of all nations. Their education, training, and participation in politics must increase so that only those too young or disabled would be excused from playing a role in such matters. The design of the process, including more than voting, would support the involvement of all those able to participate. It would operate not by some national enforcement but by a growing sense of its importance for all individuals and communities and caring for them in solidarity with neighbors.

CHAPTER 8

Rewarding Practitioners of True Democracy

One of the most important features of a democracy is participation by its citizens. Awareness of the political condition of the nation, region, and locality, self-education about these matters and their best governance, and voting all advance democracy when they characterize all capable citizens. Citizenship comes with rights. It also comes with duties. In a democracy, voting is sometimes offered as the sole duty. But simply voting does not help govern a society well unless the vote cast results from understanding the consequences of its being part of a majority.

The failure of a large percentage of citizens to vote can indicate apathy on their part. It can come from the sense that one's vote being only one among many has few consequences. It can also come from beliefs that the nation is ruled by autocrats and that democracy is simply a corrupted procedure for keeping them in power. It may result from not caring about the outcome of an election because the nonvoter has not learned about the qualifications of candidates and proposed measures. But whatever the reason, failure to vote has become a concern in this country.

Another reason may be the busy lives so many of us live. Taking time to become informed and more time to cast a ballot may seem just too much for those who must deal with raising children, working long hours, and dealing with home maintenance. Our lives are more complex now. The movement to simplify lives could help a great deal. Would adding political participation simply counter the effort to reach a simpler life?

How can that be changed? How can we have a nation of informed voters casting ballots based on knowledge and concern for the common good? How can we increase their knowledge of political matters and the characteristics of good government? We have taken the position that informing the public is a duty of elected and appointed officials. We have not included political education in the curriculum of public elementary and secondary schools probably because to do so might promote more partisanship than understanding.

Schools should have a role in educating students about the general principles of government and the nature of democracy. Teachers can be disciplined to avoid bringing up the positions of candidates and legislative proponents. I would accept the teaching of a book like *A People's History of the United States* by Howard Zinn; it points out the fact that much of the country's history does not get taught and that teaching it would have major effects on the governance of the country and likely benefits to most people.

There are probably other works that could be included along with lecturing to help accomplish this goal without engaging the students in partisanship. The teaching of democracy at home[101] and in school is documented in a number of places on the web.[102]

---

[101] See "Democracy Begins at Home" in familyeducation.com/life/parent-child-relationships/democracy-begins-home.

[102] A list of resources with links is at scholar.google.com/scholar?q=teaching+democracy+in+primary+schools&hl=en&as_sdt=0&as_vis=1&oi=scholart.

Another approach would be to reward citizens who vote regularly. We could even consider ways to sanction those who do not. Such matters could be handled through taxation laws. Citizens who vote might receive a tax reduction and those who do not might receive a tax penalty. While government need not be the source of encouraging participation, it could play a role. It might be better to have this done by private organizations acting within the law. But the government involvement would have the benefit of access to polls to document who has voted. Local parts of political parties are already allowed to do this. Given a high awareness of the costs of nonparticipation and the rewards for participation, those who do not let poll workers know their identities would change their habit. It would help if representatives of different parties or a nonpartisan group carried out a plan to do the collecting of such information.

We should note that the secret ballot rule applies to the contents of each used ballot, not to the identity of voters. We would preserve the former and seek to eliminate the latter. That one voted could be known by one's neighbors and by an agency for encouraging participation.

If private agencies were the focus of encouraging voting, how would they reward voters? I would not want financial rewards. They could lead to corruption of democracy by the intrusion of the wealthy into the process.

The "I Voted" label appears to be one way of encouraging people to vote. Some voters do not take one or wear one. And with the polls being open for more days now, people might not want to wear one every day during the election. With more people voting by mail, they don't have a label to wear. So, this idea appears to offer little in the way of encouraging more participation though some may respond to it.

How about a lottery paying something besides money? Each voter could pick up a lottery form before leaving the polling place or fill out one online or found in the vote-by-mail envelope and post it with the ballot. Several of the lottery forms could be pulled from a hat, and those picked would receive some form of laudatory publicity. It would identify them without telling how they voted but praise them as good citizens. To avoid being included in publicity, one simply can choose not to fill out and return the form. Again, the use of money as a reward could corrupt democracy.

Another possibility would involve publicizing the voter turnout rate in each area served by a polling place. It would have to include the votes cast by mail but would let a community know how well it was doing in getting out the vote. I believe such data may already be available. It would answer the question, how responsible as participating citizens are you and your neighbors? There are already websites that provide information about localities, some even suggesting that a particular town or city is a good place to live and giving reasons for that. In addition to the nonpolitical reasons, a community's percent of voter participation would give to actual and prospective residents an awareness of the level of responsibility for good citizenship to be found there and encourage residents to participate, not only as well-informed voters, but also as proponents of participation by others.

The real reward for voting is a more democratic society, so giving personal rewards may not be the answer. As individuals, we benefit from democracy and from our participation in it far more than we would from any invented reward. Perhaps the answer would come in reminding people of the benefit they receive, the benefits they provide for their neighbors, and the possibility of lasting benefits for their descendants. Keeping that information in the public realm along with the truth about actual voting would change the nation from one falsely taught that this is a great country because of its democracy to one in which citizens would have a knowledge of its truth or falsehood.

A major reward for voting could come in making voting easier. Potential voters face long lines, too few polling places, short periods of open polls, and other problems. Eliminating those problems and helping voters get to the polls would allow people to feel rewarded just by voting. It would show that they have the wisdom to take advantage of a better system and to do so in conjunction with their neighbors. Citizens who fail to vote would feel they have lost an excuse for not voting and would not want to be among the few who neglect their civic duty when it has been made easier to act.

A combination of rewards could be a better answer. Having several designed to cover the variety of situations that now contribute to low turnout would increase the likelihood that more people would turn out. Even a few personal rewards could be justified if they don't dominate the reward processes.

Another possibility would be the collection of voting data showing an individual's history. The named person hasn't missed an election in so many years. It would need to be adjusted to consider the short voting history of young people, but that could be made simple by including that information in the announcement. Remember that because people relocate, their histories would have to move with them. If that didn't happen, another means of treating them as new voters would be needed. A new voter registration period could do the trick.

Another possible reward for regular voting and having that fact recorded could be applying it to those who run for office. It could be part of the publicity candidates provide, and by their telling potential constituents of their record of political and citizen responsibility, they could gain votes. It could do so reasonably because besides a record of casting ballots, the candidate's voting record implies that she has spent time learning about qualifications for office, values of the society, and desirability of certain proposed new laws. Some candidates now reveal how they have voted. Did they vote for someone who won an office and proved to be an excellent official? They also describe why they voted for legislation to show the sort of laws they supported and continue to support. For those seeking higher office, the information would reach a wider electorate and become part of a candidate's legacy.

Voters could keep records like these on their own. That would prevent their records from being hacked or misused politically. Then, they could keep them private, share them with family and neighbors, or use them as candidates.

For those who do not run for office, being identified as responsible citizens has another value; it tells their children that society sees their participation in politics as a value. That would reinforce the lesson parents teach their children about the importance of democracy and their participation in it. In addition to adding to the respect children would have for such parents, it would remind them that they too should follow their example when they reach voting age. As they approach that age, they could begin learning more about the political system and how it affects people. Building on such knowledge for several years would prepare them to enter the world of active political participation with a desirable attitude and a fund of knowledge.

One lesson the young could learn would be that those who have been telling us a false version of our history as documented by Howard Zinn have been wrong. They would come to understand that information is available to confirm the period of inequality we have had imposed on us, and that the power of genuine democracy, including greater participation in elections, can replace inequality with greater opportunity for all. Over time, the young could see a change in our history brought about by citizens taking more responsibility and denying the wealthy of the power of autocracy.

Such a reward for society could have other benefits. One would be that it shows the error of those who claim that concentrated power is better for society. They maintain that ordinary people lack the intelligence and knowledge that would qualify them to be political decision makers and that, unlike them, their wealth shows them to be the ones who have those qualities. Such a platonic position continues to be asserted today. It has corrupted our politics and our large businesses. It continues because democracy has been choked off and has caused our society to have many people who lack the ability necessary for building better lives. That they have the potential to develop such abilities under a more democratic system needs to be shown and can be with the help of a system like the Family Independence Initiative (now Up Together).

The experience of Mauricio Miller suggests another possible reward for increasing participation. Jerry Brown, while mayor of Oakland before becoming governor of California, asked Miller what he would do to make a real difference in the lives of the poor, what he could do besides taking part in a system that raised money and used it to hire social workers. After about a month of thinking about that, he proposed to the mayor a plan that eventually became the Family Independence Initiative.

Another occurrence led to further change for Miller. President Clinton invited him in 1998 to attend his State of the Union address and to sit with others who would be introduced to the nation. He was not mentioned in the president's speech, but he met with the president and first lady and other guests in a private meeting at the White House. That had a lasting effect on him and was included in his book *The Alternative: Most of What You Believe about Poverty Is Wrong.* These events can be viewed as rewards for Miller's actions in that they motivated him to continue his work and to modify it to shift his effort from handing out money to the poor to helping the poor organize themselves and by their own efforts get out of poverty and no longer need handouts.

His book implies that his work in Oakland was rewarded by the attention of a mayor and president. Apply his story to those who successfully encourage others to register to vote, to become informed about the candidates and issues, and to follow up by casting their votes regularly. Receiving recognition from people in high places would be a reward for their actions, and it would encourage others to behave similarly. That has happened with Up Together.

So, people in positions of authority can become involved in a movement to increase citizen participation by advocating it and by bringing attention to those who are most actively involved in encouraging it in more-organized ways with their contacts with neighbors and communities. They can help the people rule.

The people *should* rule their families, cities, states, and nation. When we reach the stage at which we can say that the people are doing this, we can also say that the people are the most important part of government. In *Here the People Rule*, Richard Parker takes that position. A populist position clarifies how a constitution applies in the governing process. It allows us to say that the people are government when democracy, properly understood as a populist reality, has taken its place as the dominant feature of government.

When individuals know they play a part with others in ruling, they consider that a reward. It tells the individual that he or she is an important participant in the area of life that affects others on many levels. When done with care for others, it raises awareness of one's and others' dignity. It goes beyond just knowing and obeying laws; it reminds everyone that they have a right to share in making and improving the laws, from the most local ordinances to national constitutions. It reminds people to say, "I am important in society, and other people are too. We rule by right and obligation. We should do it as well as we can. We should do it for the benefit of all." Such a psychological reward encourages continued participation and helps keep it beneficial to the people, not just the elite.

Since many of these approaches to rewarding democratic participation have not been tested, it would be wise for some organizations to begin taking up one or a few of them, documenting their existence, and tracking their application to develop the knowledge of how well they work. While we keep in mind that the greatest reward of democracy is its service to ordinary people who now are suffering its lack, that fact can be part of every study of the rewards of participation.

Because of the continuing history of social, political, and economic corruption in the US, we have been offered reason to believe that ordinary people cannot rule well. But let us challenge that belief. Let us put it to the test of building respect for the potential rewards of participation by increasing everyone's participation.

We are not talking about a perfect society, just a better one. We should want it to be better for those who suffer most from its greatest imperfections, neglect of the poor, concentration of wealth, and enforced servitude through unfair employment practices.

In its social teaching, the Roman Catholic Church advocates the preferential option for the poor. That happens when donations are made to them to relieve their poverty. But unless the donations are part of a continuing practice, we give reason to the saying, "The poor we always have with us." I believe that saying is true even in the most just societies, but in those societies, the poor would be few and not remain in poverty for long. They might be the victims of health problems, accidents, or personal mistakes, but they would not remain in that state except in the sense that they would not have wealth or be able to manage it for their benefit. Bad physical or mental health could put them in that position. They would have to be cared for by others and should be. So, they are poor only in the sense that they cannot do for themselves economically what others can do, but they would not suffer poverty or inadequate diets, homelessness, or isolation.

They might be unable to take part in political government. Seeing that as a terrible loss for a person can help us to see the value of participation for those who can. By bringing to communities more of the work based on the strategy of Mauricio Miller and applying it to citizen participation as he applied it to poverty could benefit them in numerous ways. One way would be to show them that they have the power to influence government when they become active in politics in conjunction with their neighbors. It would help them to escape poverty by becoming an influence in the political sphere and using that influence to reduce the power of the elite and super wealthy. In doing that, they would help others learn to do the same. They would learn the power of cooperation with their neighbors and make it an important part of their lives. And they would learn from their neighbors more about the policies that are good for the community and the larger political environment.

Does this mean that people would no longer take different political positions? Not really. But the current deeply divided nation, taking its positions by partisanship and not by knowledge of social and political realities, would find its differences in elections reduced to less divisive choices. They might differ in minor ways involving efficiency or timeliness of some measures and greater appreciation of the skills and attitudes of one candidate over those of another.

In the next chapter, we will show how politics based on the values that benefit communities would help promote peace there and in the larger entities, leading to world peace, a state we need to attain and preserve. As more people worldwide come to see the threat of human annihilation from the deep flaws in the current way of life, they will insist more than ever that the people should rule and that their demands must be carried out on all levels of government that have responsibility for them.

CHAPTER 9

A World at Peace

The values we seek when we understand human nature and the good life for all are many. The context of this work could include them all, but because one value has become critical to our survival as a species, I have chosen to focus on it in this chapter as the most needed consequence of genuine democracy. Peace stands out because if we don't achieve it, we will lack other needed values and their lack will contribute to our destruction.

Militarism, a worldwide fault we must overcome, threatens our existence. Despite our having learned that nuclear weapons can cause death and destruction on a scale we deplore, we go on creating them. The Little Boy bomb dropped on Hiroshima had the explosive power of 15,000 tons of TNT, many times the power of earlier bombs. The Fat Man bomb exploded on Nagasaki with the power of 21,000 tons of TNT. A hydrogen bomb typically has the explosive and destructive power of 1,000 atomic bombs. Although no nuclear bombs have been used since the first two in Japan, the world remains threatened by a continuing history of their development in nations hostile to one another. The cost in human effort and financial support wastes important elements needed for a better life in many nations.

Other deadly weapons developed since World War II have been an ongoing tragedy for many people, particularly in the Middle East. Tanks have been made more capable of use in terrains hard to cross in earlier versions. Missiles now target cities, planes, and other missiles. Drones provide observation and attack on vehicles, buildings, and individuals while their controllers may sit half a world away from their targets. And soldier-borne weapons have become more deadly and accurate, making the sniper and the line soldier a threat to any enemy. And now China and the US are beginning to explore and develop a future with weapons in space.

The wars in Latin America and the Middle East have taken the lives of many military personnel and civilians. The development of militarism continues in the most wealthy and powerful nation in the world, the US. It serves as an example for smaller and weaker nations that devote much of their economic power to the development of weapons including nuclear, and to the sustaining of military forces to use conventional weapons.

Wars go on. The US withdrew from Afghanistan, where it had conducted war for twenty years, the longest war in our history. It has left a nation in a state of starvation and destruction not so very different from that of Iran and Yemen, where children are starving and families are fleeing, becoming refugees in places where they are not welcomed. The tragedy continues. And now Russia has invaded Ukraine after surrounding the nation with over 150,000 troops and many deadly weapons. Its action has prompted NATO and the US to promise bad consequences for Russia. The earlier vague Russian threats included warnings of military action against any nation attempting to use its military strength to oppose what Russia was doing. We see the evidence for that in the buildup of forces in Ukraine and the movement of American forces to the area. The nightly news covers the story by showing the threats being made by national leaders and the opinions of many foreign relations experts.

A world in which war continues to take and degrade human lives must not continue as it has for many years. We must find ways to promote peace and prosperity for all people even though that will mean living in different ways with values different from those that have marked us for so long. The militarism of wealthy nations must be replaced by policies that promote peace by building trust between all nations and by ending the economic exploitation of the weak.

American militarism is the highest in the world. We have troops in nearly 800 bases in over eighty countries and allow no foreign nations to station their troops in ours. We have approximately 490 naval ships at sea or in reserve and more planned and under construction. We think that having the most powerful military force in the world makes our people safe. We spend a huge amount of money on our defense budget, over $700 billion in 2021, about a sixth of the national budget. It is more than the next ten other largest military budgets in the world combined. Because our military capabilities and deployment around the world appear as a threat to many nations, they will not give up their own military forces, some still having nuclear weapons. We give them the reason to spend money and human effort needed for other aspects of human life on military development. Doing that, they then give us the excuse to do the same. That we choose to do it on a scale so much larger than any one of theirs should make us ask why.

And now we are being asked to militarize near space, to create and deploy weapons to carry on war above the atmosphere and bring it down to earth. The cost and danger of such a practice adds further to the need to get over the idea that creating more deadly weapons makes us safe. Aside from the danger of such weapons from their potential use, they add to the millions of pieces of space junk circling the earth and threatening to fall onto the earth at places where people could be harmed, and property destroyed. That we have no international program to clean up the junk shows the shortsightedness caused by militarism.

We must find ways to end our militarism and together with other nations theirs as well. It must become a common strategy for allowing peace to replace the horrible events that have marked modern times and threaten to end human life. We should find ways to reduce the power of nations to conduct large-scale warfare. That would involve a worldwide process of eliminating nuclear and other very deadly weapons and reducing the size of militaries to the point that they would be unable to carry on wars against their neighbors let alone a world war. The value of their time and effort would move from military bases and ships to their homes, where they would contribute to better family and community lives. It would be a better life for them as well, a fact that should be made well known by those who first make the move.

Before we can get rid of the world's weapons, we must build the relations of trust and mutual concern that would allow us to see militarism as needless and harmful.

We need to come to understand solidarity and how to make it grow between ourselves and those we classify as enemies. We must take the words of George Washington and Dwight Eisenhower seriously. We must first have the desire to have no national enemies. Making such a desire a reality would have enormous economic benefits and allow us to deal with our internal inequities. We see the complexity of the problem in the desire of some Americans to gain great wealth at the expense of others. They can change their view, but it will take time and a good deal of effort educating people to the horrors of our present system. Eisenhower's advice to give up the military-industrial complex would free up many people with technical and scientific education and skills and allow them to devote their talents, energies, and time to producing safe and helpful products and services.

A most interesting work by Carlos Eduardo Maldonado, *Human Rights, Solidarity, and Subsidiarity*,[103] places major importance on civil society and the power of nongovernmental organizations to make major changes in the world of human organization and to achieve changes that will lead to gaining and preserving peace. Regarding democracy, he notes, "Democracy in its most radical or root form is participative democracy—not simply representative or merely deliberative democracy."[104]

---

[103] This short but important work can be read online at http://www.crvp.org/publications/Series-V/5-Contents.pdf. An article by Domènec Melé, "The Principle of Subsidiarity in Organizations: A Case Study," outlines the principles for applying subsidiarity to organizations such as businesses and gives an encouraging example of its success in the Spanish social insurance business, Fremap. View at deliverypdf.ssrn.com/delivery.php?ID=363114095103068021072093084029092100127044006079024031064085064000111114071027082085099050107020030120050076076113113067123006006038011067027113064005086005106008033024095014121119094107113084116112023115015005028112029002024083122126084084124098&EXT=pdf&INDEX=TRUE.

[104] Ibid., 44. On intersubjectivity, see *I and Thou* by Martin Buber.

He goes on to develop his view of subsidiarity as two different concepts, one a political formation as in the European Union and the other as an ethical principle of organizing for the benefit of people, the view I hold.

Solidarity with family and friends takes place for most people, but solidarity with people in other nations, even those considered to be allies of ours, does not often occur. Yet there are ways to bring it about.

One experience changed my view of China and gave me a sense of solidarity with the Chinese people. Michael Wood presented a series of television shows about other nations. I was particularly impressed with one that featured Italy and its history and another that dealt with China and its history, a subject we are not generally taught except for the more recent times when China adopted Communism. After viewing the latter, I had a greatly changed view of the Chinese people and their progress as a society. Some of their leaders were exemplary, and some of their social movements were too. It made me realize that their recent history need not be the sole basis for understanding them and that they can bring about changes that can make them a major contributor to good relations with others including us. I have no idea how many others reacted to the video the way I did, but there must be some. And the video should be available for those who have not seen it yet.

That lesson and studying other examples of civil society in foreign nations has affected my view of a world that has much to teach us. Simply taking our nation as the best in the world and believing that all others are inferior has blinded us to important lessons we can learn from them. Studying Italy and Mondragon as examples of well-developed societies with worker cooperatives would add much to our knowledge of how to achieve economic equality and make democracy a true practice in daily life.

Other European nations have a good deal to teach us as well. Sweden, Norway, and the Netherlands deserve to be studied so that we may better understand why they are rated toward the top of nations in some of the most important categories of human happiness. Besides teaching us how to improve our government and economy, it would increase our solidarity with the people there and help us come to understand them as more than just military allies. It would help us achieve what President Washington advised in his farewell address. We should avoid the sort of permanent friendships with other nations that involve taking their enemies to be our enemies. We should work to resolve differences with nations we consider opponents.

How can we do that? As with any large movement, it must begin with understanding. We must understand what harm the military-industrial complex has created and the dangers of allowing it to continue. We must understand how threatening other people with our weapons motivates them to develop their own weapons so that they can defend themselves with threats to us and if necessary, with their use. We must understand how our economic behavior toward them has given them reason to distrust us. We must understand how solidarity with them would help them and us in ways that we haven't imagined.

Given a higher level of understanding, we might begin by improving our trade relations with poor countries. We would cease to look for ways to take advantage of their poverty, low taxes, and low wages by moving our businesses there and operating them in a way that keeps their workers poor and some Americans rich. We would give up the practice of shipping our industrially produced farm products to them and putting their local farmers out of business. As advised in *Economic Justice for All*, we would buy from them only products that they produce and that we can't and vice versa.

What we ship overseas should be products that others need, not simply products that we happen to make and want to sell. We would stop competing with them for world markets and make trade the beneficial practice that it can be. We would engage in what *Economic Justice for All* calls balanced trade; it harms no one and benefits the trading partners. It is a form of cooperation that would replace the harmful deception and domination by the World Bank and the other organizations (the International Monetary Fund and the World Trade Organization) formed as a result of the Bretton Woods conference. Such organizations have proven to be of greater harm to poor nations than the help they claimed they would be. The IMF has made help for poor nations dependent on their having policies called austerity measures that hold their people back from economic advancement. The measures apply to the poor and require that they do without a lot they need for a good life under the name of austerity. For Americans to impose such measures on others without practicing them amounts to a form of hypocrisy that needs to be exposed and ended.

While we are working for peaceful relations with other nations, we should also be working with them to protect the environment we all depend on. That would protect and preserve the power of the earth to continue providing what we all need to live, and it would add to the appreciation of nations by one another and build the cooperation we need to sustain peace among us. It would help us end the competition for respect as "the best nation on earth" and replace it with respect for all people as dignified human beings.

E. F. Schumacher, in *Small Is Beautiful: Economics as if People Mattered*, recommends we reduce the attachment to many unneeded material things. It dominates our country and provides a strong foundation for the struggle to gain wealth at the expense of others. That struggle goes on, supported also by the suppression of information about the motives of the wealthy and the poverty it sustains for the poorest in our nation and around the world.

Schumacher and others describe a way of life simpler than what we have known in recent years. It is a way of life that does not attract some because we have been taught that progress moved us beyond it through the development of technology, the building of capitalist organizations, and the acquisition of natural resources on a scale never known before. What is described as progress turns out to be just for a few and regression for many. It has harmed those who must depend on jobs with large corporations in our country and people in other countries where the economic growth has been stifled. Here, I do not mean economic growth in the sense it is usually presented in this country: growth of the GDP and the Dow Jones stock average. I am referring to economic growth in the many homes where people must live, obtain food and clothing, raise and educate children, and sustain local infrastructure. It is economic growth from the bottom up and particularly for the poor. If they do not experience economic growth, there is no reason to speak of growth as a good thing no matter how much the high-level accounting numbers grow.

That growth would not be to make the poor wealthy but to lift them out of poverty in a sustainable way. Nor is economic growth achieved by damaging the environment a cause for celebration. It will lead to human destruction and an environment that can no longer sustain life.

The Catholic Church's social teaching advocates reducing greed as more than a pragmatic value for reducing environmental damage. It presents it as a moral basis for any good human life that being neglected in greed is a sin that causes many to suffer. It shows it to be one of the most important teachings of Jesus verbally and in the example he set by the way he lived.

Other religions have taught the lesson as well. The Jewish faith inherited by Jesus made condemnation of greed a major value frequently presented in its teaching. Other religions teach us to collect and use matter only as needed for the good life. Buddhism has it as a major topic. Buddhism also has a major theme against violence. In his work, Maldonado sees in violence the attack on humanity, not just on individuals. It also makes greed the cause of most violence.

As does Christianity, Buddhism promotes a spiritual life that puts our material needs and their satisfaction in their proper place in our lives, providing the opportunity to live a good life with others in reciprocity and solidarity. It tells us that we must see others as we see ourselves and to see them and ourselves together as having the same dignity. It requires that we cooperate and share, producing only enough to make that possible for supporting life and for enjoyment of life in work, leisure, creativity, and learning. What we all learn need not be how to make a more marketable automobile but the shared nature of humanity and its capabilities for development as a loving, responsible species caring for all humans and the environment. Such a society would enjoy peace individually, locally, nationally, and internationally and pass that on.

The differences in religions would no longer cause violence in which the faithful of one religion seek to destroy those who do not share their belief. The ecumenism and advocacy of religious freedom brought out by the Second Vatican Council have echoes in other faiths, particularly Buddhism. The Thirty Years' War in the Holy Roman Empire grew out of religious differences and the struggle for imperial power between the Hapsburgs in Austria and Spain and French House of Bourbon. The current warfare between Jewish people and Muslim Palestinians in the Middle East must have more to do with imperialism than simply religious differences. These two examples show us that religious differences alone should not entitle us to go to war or condemn people of different faiths. The Treaty of Westphalia that settled the Thirty Years' War exposed the imperialism of participating nations by making the politically powerful in each of them the ones to determine the religion of their people and not the people themselves.[105]

The current move among nations, including the US, to move political power from the national government when appropriate and place it in the local governments has been described as decentralization. Based on the desire for localism and a greater experience of democracy, decentralization has become a reality in many countries but not so much in the US. That is why we must

---

[105] The doctrine expressed as *Cuius regio, eius religio* gave the power to determine a nation's religion to its ruler.

come to understand the need for it and the values it would bring to life here. To do that, we need to understand subsidiarity and the relationship between it and decentralization.

In the European Union, subsidiarity has been a reality for some time. Since it is a part of the European Union Treaty signed at Maastricht in 1992, it has shaped the relations between the member nations and the EU. It must also have made European people in the member states aware of subsidiarity as they are not in the US. But in the EU, subsidiarity is treated as a practical matter, having its origin and meaning in the treaty that gave rise to it and describes its application. In Catholic social teaching, subsidiarity has a different meaning. Various encyclicals discuss the practical need for it, but its basis is not some treaty but an ethical requirement.

One effect of the difference is to make the application of subsidiarity as described in Catholic social teaching a broader concept. That is, it applies not just to the relation between one higher authority and a lower one as it does in the EU. Properly understood, it applies to many more relationships, even to all local communities and families, to the states of the US and the cities in those states, and even to global corporations and their local establishments.

As an ethical requirement, subsidiarity gives a different meaning to localism and democracy. It should make us realize the moral need of individuals and local groups to study the needs of people and how they can be met more locally, especially when attempting to meet them through a national authority fails and ends up serving the greed of a few in an institutional way. This is not to accuse all owners of stock of being personally greedy but to recognize that the system we have can serve them if they are. This is not the case with localism and subsidiarity. The moral principle prevents the power of a higher authority from succumbing to greed or enabling it for the managers of major corporations. It means that we must be aware of how local needs can be met and when they can't be met through local action. Only then does a matter fall into the hands of a higher authority. And when it does, that higher authority must, to remain ethical, meet the need of the subsidiary group in a way that preserves its authority over other matters, those it can handle locally.

The ethical basis of subsidiarity should be made well known to the people of the world and especially the people of the US. Its effects in application should be presented clearly and truthfully in sufficient detail so that people can understand it and judge when it is being observed and when it is being neglected. Reaching that level of public understanding would allow it to become a part of the political structure that would include legislation and juridical traditions, making its violation a cause for legal punishment.

We see that it has not reached that stage, even in the EU and certainly not in the US. Its being less known and not at all enacted in the US has resulted in our country trailing Europe in political, economic, and social development. And we trail them in the reality of our democracy. Each of these would be improved if the topic became a widespread demand for change here. Its effect on localism and democracy should be made a part of a long national discussion out of which would arise the will to make the change. And out of the change would arise a truer democracy with its benefits for the lives of people, reduction of poverty, development of education, and power of the people.

How would that promote peace? One way concerns the development of societies in terms of the distribution of the orders of consciousness. A society in which many people do not develop beyond imperial consciousness becomes a dangerous and harmful society. Such a society thrives on domination, a sense of justice limited to retributive, and the use of violence to achieve its goals.

Korten sees as a goal a global community held together by values promoted by a world full of people with the three later orders of consciousness. Those with social consciousness would act as a swing vote between the imperial and the cultural. The cultural would be inspired by those few who exhibit spiritual consciousness. Korten gives examples of the latter as Jesus, Gandhi, Buddha, and Martin Luther King Jr. They inspire people to seek truth, justice, and concern for others regardless of race or religious beliefs and to care for the environment. While we need the teachings of those whom Korten names, we also need to have some in each generation develop to that level in order to bring light to their contemporary issues and possibilities.

Above all, we need to see those who have reached the imperial level develop beyond it. Because they are the promoters of militancy, social domination, and subjugating capitalism, they are far too influential in our country. We must find a way to help them move to the next level and from there to the cultural level. When that occurs with great abundance in a society, its values change. It can embrace peaceful resolution of differences, reduced competition, and greater cooperation to achieve desirable goals. The goals as well will be improved so that cooperation that becomes conspiracy will no longer be as evident as it is now.

Key to the improvement of a society's distribution of the

higher levels of consciousness, education should change so that it begins to make the young aware of the possibility of their developing into the higher levels and to see the better leaders as examples of what they can become even if they do not devote their lives to becoming great leaders themselves. For them to become good parents, participating citizens in a well-directed democracy, and cooperators with neighbors in building and maintaining a desirable community, all these are goals that can be taught and should be learned gradually and to greater depth as people age. It should become our understanding that maturity is important and has many faces but is guided by principles and values we learn as we age. And it should not occur just in old age. Maturity can develop with the training and should be seen at each stage of adulthood. While being aided by the example of others, individuals can contribute to their own development from early adulthood on.

CONCLUSION

The development in practice of the three themes of this book—subsidiarity, localism, and true democracy—will lead to sustainable peace in local areas, nations, regions, and in the world. Other social, economic, and political improvements will also contribute to peace. For example, a wide use of social media will allow people in different countries to discover one another and to communicate to the point that would resemble the earlier pen pal custom; friendships develop out of such interaction. Since people do not want their friends to be threatened with domination or war, they will use their greater democratic power to influence government to eliminate any position of continuing adversity with their friends' nations.

As the US becomes a nation of greater equality between races and genders as it is now doing, the high poverty rate of African Americans, women, and indigenous people will decline and allow them to have better education, more leisure, and more political participation. Given their sensitivity to the need for equity born of their history of mistreatment, they will become an even more active source of social and political organization and increase economic and social equality while reducing the fear that motivates militarism. Now that we have a vice president of mixed race including black, and a new black, female member of the Supreme Court for the first time, they will show the way to set aside the preference for an all-white, male government and the attitudes of superiority of the race and gender that underlie it.

Finally, a growing appreciation for nature and the preservation of wildlife will strengthen the determination to eliminate the use of highly destructive weapons and the militaristic attitudes encouraging their development and deployment. Peace among nations will increase as more people participate in the movement to make it a reality. It is up to all of us to see that governments turn away from war and adopt interstate improvements that this and future generations in all countries can support.

Printed in the United States
by Baker & Taylor Publisher Services